MW01596139

Priorities…

First Edition Design Publishing
Sarasota, Florida

Priorities...
Copyright ©2015 Elizabeth Stuart-Grimes

ISBN 978-1622-878-47-5 PRINT
ISBN 978-1622-877-48-2 EBOOK

LCCN 2015933957

April 2015

Published and Distributed by
First Edition Design Publishing, Inc.
P.O. Box 20217, Sarasota, FL 34276-3217
www.firsteditiondesignpublishing.com

"<u>Priorities...</u>"was originally written in early 2003 but – due to the need to pay the rent and monthly bills – the author went back to work. It is now available to the public because the author has taken a much needed rest (known as a writer's sabbatical) to finish this work.

For Lacy

Happy Reading !

Elizabeth

Priorities…

*Understanding the difference between
what we want and what we need.*

Elizabeth Stuart-Grimes

"I am, no more, no less, the reincarnation of the collective voice of my ancestors put back on Earth to teach my children and my children's children what is important to learn in the brief period that we all call 'a life'. I have, however, taken advantage of this time to observe and learn by watching others and to interpret my observations and lessons into the tales told by those who have gone before me."

Elizabeth Stuart-Grimes

Thanks go to...

Well, first, thank you to my family: my husband and my children, and to my close friends who put up with me and encouraged me.

To my mother, Margaret, and my dad, Robert, who have always been and will always be proud of me...wherever they are.

To my oldest friend, Carol, the person who knows me better than anyone and who also happens to be the best editor a writer could hope for!

To my friends, friends of friends, and some family who have shared their stories with me so I could share them: thank you. All the names and places have been changed to protect your privacy.

To my 'Supreme Beings', my angels, my elders, my guides, for always pointing me in the right directions and for catching me when I have fallen. I know who you are and I thank you all; and I know you are there for me. (*And to those of you who had to push REALLY hard to make me understand: thank you, but could you push a little less dramatically? I promise I'll listen more carefully from now on...*)

My brief Introduction

This recitation, for that's exactly what it is, is meant to remind you what it was like to sit and listen to an old auntie or grandparent. The transfer of information from one generation to another has lost its soul, its personality. Long before internet and social media, emails, faxes, computers, typewriters, or even pen and ink, life's lessons were transmitted from our elders to the young through stories…and that's what this collection is: stories.

There are stories about the young and the old; there are stories about the middle years.

You may like reading something that sounds like someone speaking just to you. You may not. I will not take it personally if you don't. I do, however, hope you learn something because that's what this is all about. It's not Confucius or Lao Tse. It's just common, day-to-day experiences about real people that may or may not relate to the world that you are currently living in.

This book is about finding the priorities in your life. It will try to show you the difference between what you want and what you need.

I hope you enjoy it.

Priorities…

Elizabeth Stuart-Grimes

Table of Contents

Priorities: Want or Need

My world in 1980

"I grew up at the end of the age of the baby boomers. I went to school. I graduated from high school. I went to the college of my choice. My parents paid the bills. I went to work in New York City. I got my own apartment and I paid my bills as well as I could.

That's life.

New York City – like any big city in the 1980s – was a world in itself. Everything was rush, rush, rush. If your bosses wanted something done, they wanted it yesterday. We were expected to be able to do everything and anything. When a client asked if something extraordinary was possible, our answer was always, "Of course; that's not a problem" we would figure out how to do it after the client went back home.

We worked hard and we played hard. It was the era of nightclubs such as Studio 54, Limelight, and Area. We worked all day, danced and drank until the wee hours of morning, got a few hours of sleep, and were back at the office again. When we were too tired to go out, we became 'couch potatoes'.

One of my clearest memories was sitting down in the plush conference room in my company's advertising agency in one of the towers on Avenue of the Americas and watching all the executives file in; take out their chic leather daily agendas; place their expensive Tiffany, Cartier, or Mont Blanc pens next to their note pads; smooth their Hermes ties correctly; check their gold watches; and sit back to wait for the meeting to begin. The women executives went through the same routine except they readjusted their silk scarves and tugged at their suit sleeves so that everyone could see the elegant bracelets they were wearing. These were our marks: What we wore, what we carried with us, and how we behaved. Was it all necessary? Of course!

I was ever so surprised to find out that my account manager, a good looking young fellow in his early thirties, actually lived about two blocks from me on York Avenue in an apartment almost as small as my own. We had worked together for almost two years and we were neighbors! Yet that was work and our private lives didn't enter into it. What amused me was that I wasn't the only person, it seemed, in this enormous company that sold "Luxury" who lived alone in approximately 250 square feet furnished with old furniture that had belonged to the grandparents, a few things picked up at IKEA, and bric-a-brac discovered at tag sales. But none of that mattered. We got up every morning; put on our expensive suits, watches, jewelry, scarves and ties, our expensive black shoes, our elegant navy blue cashmere coats; and went to work, where we sold LUXURY. We sold diamonds, we sold cars; we sold dishwashers and dishwasher detergent. We sold vacation packages, we sold gourmet food…for a while we even tried to sell hamburgers. We made money… a lot of it…, which we spent, not on us but on presenting a way of life. We believed every slogan we wrote and we lived those words.

I had mastered the art of the "no problem" response and was nicely climbing the corporate ladder. I did what I was told and I didn't make waves. I was given the responsibility for an important client based in a tiny town in Michigan on the other side of the lake from Chicago. They often came to New York for meetings with their prestigious advertising agency – "Of course," I thought, "They want to get out of that little hole they live in and come to the REAL city." How wrong I was.

Very soon after my assignment to this client, I was informed that I was to fly out there to meet the whole team so that I would get a better idea of how the company functioned. I flew to Chicago – business class – and then went to another terminal to catch the little twin-engine hopper that would take me across the lake. Other than the fact that I don't like little planes, nothing had prepared me for this trip. I arrived and was greeted by one of my new "team" members who was extremely pleasant and helped me with my chic little MoMA black bag and leather briefcase. (Author's note: in the 1980's you could buy a black canvas and leather satchel at the Museum of Modern Art for a reasonable price.) She drove me in her little American-made car to my motel where my room was already paid for and then we went to the office – a red brick building that was remodeled from an old 1950s elementary school. Driving to the office, we passed houses that I thought should have been torn down decades ago – this was really the sticks – old cars decaying in backyards, dogs tied to doghouses...

Everything I had been indoctrinated to dislike and avoid because I was selling 'Luxury'.

The flaw in my education within the advertising and marketing world was that we targeted our work on what influenced the USA's major market areas and assumed that the rest just followed along. If it didn't happen in New York, Los Angeles, or Chicago, could it really matter? We assumed (wrongly, I might add) that the people who lived outside of these areas wanted to be just like the people who lived in them. What I discovered was that most of the people who lived outside the major target markets actually made a calculated choice to do so. They were highly intelligent, well educated people who simply didn't want to live their lives being assaulted by the rushed, quasi-violent world of major industrialized cities.

My day-to-day client contact was a young woman named Sarah who had majored in Home Economics at Ohio State University. She was great. She was proud of her education, thrilled with her job, and really good at it. She might have been happy living in a major city, but she was just as happy living in this tiny town. She didn't have an MBA, but she didn't need one. She didn't drive a fancy foreign car because she didn't need to. If she wanted to go to the theater or to see a museum exhibit, she went while she was in Chicago or New York on business. Her life was no less fulfilled than mine or anyone else's. She had found a job that she enjoyed and that she did well, and that's what was important to her at that period in her life.

What hit me the hardest was that meeting business people outside of my "world" was destabilizing what I had been trained to do at work. I started to make the connection between Sarah and my mother. When Sarah told me that she was graduated from Ohio State, it jolted me into reality. My mother had gone to Ohio State (and had been a Home Economics major). My mother is a fabulous woman who runs major fundraising events for charities and public 'government' events. A woman who always carries herself with so much self-assurance. A woman who grew up in Middle America but – to me, the big city kid – never showed her origins.

I was wrong...so very wrong, and I was ashamed at what a snob I had become. Luckily I learned this when I was relatively young. Sarah was like me, like my mother, like so many millions of other women who grew up in "Middle America" who were well-educated, well-rounded, intelligent...

The ice that had broken off of my iceberg was starting to melt.

By the end of my three-day trip, I had learned more than in ten years working in the ad agency, and I went back to "the City" with a huge chip on my shoulder. We had to stop talking about America as if it were only New York, Chicago, and Los Angeles. These cities were NOT the real world...the real world was "out there" in between all that. I had suddenly realized that we didn't know for whom we were writing all this luxurious advertising at all.

That chip on my shoulder ultimately cost me my place in the New York advertising world but that didn't matter to me anymore. The clients that I left behind when I moved out of New York were furious because they had found in me the one thing totally lacking in the majority of advertising people...someone who told the truth. The Truth was what I found on that trip to the backwoods of Michigan and it's never left me. Stories told to me about how to treat people who work for you suddenly made sense to me because it spoke The Truth. Remarks such as "It's the little people who make the world go round..." are truths so deep that until you meet "those" people you can't really understand.

Sarah opened my eyes to the real world. I've always wondered what happened to her. Several years ago I tried finding her, but the wonders of the internet were no help. I'm sure she married and had children and is very happy with her life because it's a life that she chose based on an educated decision.

Those 'truths' that we are constantly confronted with, do they help you have a better life? My business trip to Michigan helped me see <u>my truth</u>, my way with other people, and it reminded me what my mother and some of her close friends taught me about how to act and how to treat people.

It has to do with how you treat the cashier at the little grocery store: Are you pleasant or dry to the point of almost being rude? Do you say hello to the newspaperman or do you drop the money, pick up your paper, and keep moving? Do the guys who work in the sandwich shop – you know, the ones who serve you two of your three meals a day, the ones who know how you like your coffee and which sandwich you are likely to order for lunch... those guys – do you know their names? Are you so important that you take no notice of others?

When someone comes to fix an appliance or a leaky faucet in your home, do you offer him (or her) coffee, or a beer if it's the end of the day? Do you "chat" with them or ignore them while they're working?

When I was little, my mom took my father's shirts and the dry-cleaning to the same place every week; she had a sort of relationship with all the people who worked there. Mom was always polite and cheerful with them, even when something wasn't done right – and they always said, "I'm sorry, M'am, we'll re-do it." They treated her with respect because she was respectful of them.

The people I met in the little town in Michigan were honest, incredibly intelligent, hardworking executives who had made a conscious choice not to live in big cities; not to raise their children among skyscrapers but instead with trees and grass and fresh air. They weren't any lesser people than my co-workers or I or the other people who worked in "the big city." They were people who had already put their priorities in order. Is that sort of decision a truth? I suppose yes and no, but it's most certainly a decision one makes based on life priorities.

That is, after all, what this discussion is all about: Priorities. Do you want or do you need the fancy leather agenda with your monogram embossed in gold. Look at the question again: Of course you _want_ it, but do you

NEED it? No, you don't, and that is how you define your life's priorities.

Look around you. Are there things in your home that you purchased that you could consider frivolous? If you can afford to buy "frivolous," you are doing well. It probably means that you have correctly defined certain priorities in your life. If you buy things that can be considered "frivolous" and that you can't really afford, then you need to reassess your priorities.

I have a constant reminder of "frivolous" in my bedroom: a very large gray stuffed bear purchased for far too much money during my first year out of college. I paid for him with my very own credit card and regretted it for years. I spent money on that bear that should have gone towards my rent, my student loans, and my general day-to-day costs of living.

I've kept that bear to remind me to keep my financial priorities in line; to remember to ask the question, "do I need it or do I want it" before buying something that I would otherwise consider frivolous. Priorities.

This is what we are talking about. Job priorities. Family priorities. People priorities. Life Priorities…."

My Priorities

My world in 2014

If you have gotten this far and wish to continue, welcome to my world of common sense... or at least what seems like common sense to me.

I originally wrote this book in 2002-2003. America had been through the 9/11 tragedy and the Dot Com financial crash. I had printed a dozen copies of this and distributed to friends, who all agreed it should be published.

What happened next was a 'want versus need' situation in my own life. With three children in school, we could no longer afford for me to be a full time mom. The occasional freelance writing jobs I was picking up were not enough to supplement our income. It was time to go back to work full time because we needed the money. This manuscript was shoved in a box under my desk at home and forgotten until another life altering event made me wake up.

In 2011-2012, several events shook my little world in rather rapid succession. The company I work for was sold and reorganized. I lost my high-ranking position, although I still had a job and my salary. A very good friend committed suicide. My father was diagnosed with and subsequently died from pancreatic cancer. One of my sons was experimenting with drugs and failing out of school. And then... as though someone was trying to get through to me that I wasn't paying attention to what really mattered -- that I had lost track of my life priorities -- I fell benignly from a horse and suffered a relatively significant head trauma. Everything that I had been focused on was scrambled. I couldn't communicate with my colleagues or family correctly. (I worked for a company where French and English are required on a daily basis. After my head trauma, I could no longer speak French at all.) I couldn't remember how to spell words with more than one syllable. I couldn't remember anything that had happened the day before. All the clothes in my closet were so foreign to me, I couldn't wear them. My personality had completely changed. Even my eating habits changed.

I have spent the past 2 years recuperating my life. My family and friends have stuck by me and put up with my mood swings and weird behavior.

One day after a major mistake, I went to speak with my boss and I was very blunt. I said, "You have a choice: Me at 80 percent or me on sick leave for 6 months. If I stay, I'm going to make mistakes and I'm going to forget things. You choose." Amazingly enough he chose me at 80 percent. Working helped me heal and reconnect the parts of my brain that had been damaged in the fall.

Working hard like that for a year also showed me what I was capable of. I developed a level of concentration that I didn't know existed in me. I also had the time to see what was wrong with my life's direction.

Fifteen months after my accident I had to make a decision about moving forward. I asked the management for a 1-year sabbatical. I needed a break from the company and I wanted (or perhaps *needed*) to see if I could finish the manuscript that I had shoved under my desk in 2003.

This is where I am now. I'm finishing something that I started more than 12 years ago. I'm updating a few points and adding a few chapters, but I also have noticed that what wrote 12 years ago still stands true.

Finding our priorities should be each person's number one priority. ...and it shouldn't take a fall on the head to see what's important for each and every one of us.

Daily Life

Can you honestly say that you have everything you need?

For most people, yes, you have a nice home with a lovely yard, two cars, 2.6 children, a dog or cat, the children go to good schools – perhaps private or religious schools – you have a good job, your spouse has a good job, you have nice neighbors – well, maybe one or two that you could live without. The cleaning lady is honest even though you don't understand the language she speaks. The kid who cuts the lawn seems bright enough. You get to go on vacation once a year and you were able to buy that awesome home entertainment system last year. So, yes, you have everything that you need.

Fine. Let's look at the question again in detail. What do you NEED? If you had to cut your expenses down to the bare minimum tomorrow, what do you absolutely have to have?

That's simple isn't it: You need shelter for your family, heat, food, a decent school, and, if you're lucky, a good job where you are appreciated. You don't really need more than that. The rest is gravy.

Look at the increasing amount of 'tiny homes' popping up in internet articles and deco magazines. They are people who have scaled down to live with only what they NEED.

This isn't a lecture with a moral at the end; it's a reality check, that's all. Your home is where you live with your family, whether it's a tiny apartment or a luxurious estate. You buy a house or an apartment -- you make your home. What did the grandmothers of this generation use to say? Home is where your heart is. Well, it's true.

Okay, now you have 4 square walls with a roof over them. Add heat and electricity. If you're lucky, add plumbing. Beyond that the rest is what you want but you've fulfilled the necessity part of the deal. Congratulations.

For many it's a major breakthrough. In achieving this you've made a step towards defining your priorities.

If you wish to become a gourmet cook, do it. Be aware that what is important is to eat correctly and to feed your children correctly... the rest really *is* gravy! In seeking your priorities, perspective is important too. The cost of 100 grams of Russian caviar can feed a family of 4 for several days.

If you wish to sign your kids up for little league team sports, do it. But ask yourself why you are doing it... for them, or for something you didn't achieve for yourself? Does your son really WANT to play football? Does your daughter really WANT to be on the gymnastic team?

This is not to second-guess parents who think their children will benefit from a team sport because they need to build confidence in themselves. We did it to our son who – at age seven – had a terrible time making friends, AND he needed to do a sport that helped him develop his right-left equilibrium. Did we force him for two years? Yes. Did he learn (with much difficulty) to be part of a group? Yes. Did he form friendships that, amusingly enough, he'll probably have for the rest of his life? Yes. Has he turned out to be a good team player? Yes, in fact he has realized that he works better with a team in his job.

Being part of that sports team (they weren't very good), he learned how to lose better than he learned to win. However, when they DID win, they collectively enjoyed having won together. This was a choice we made. It became a priority in our daily lives. We LIVED that team sport for more than 12 years – to the point that one of us became active in the team's parents' association and his little brother and sister also played. When our son asked to stop playing, we asked why and his reasons were valid. He was old enough to make that decision on his own. It's his life; it's his choice; it's his list of priorities (though with a little guidance from his parents!).

Do you see what I mean by daily life priorities? We could have put him on that team but not backed it up with our time. Would we have accomplished the same thing? No, I don't think so. Did we give up things to be there at every match to support him and his team? Yes and no. We gave up family time doing other things, but we were still all together as a family. Everyone went to the matches and, as already noted, his younger brother and little sister joined the team too. It was a choice we made as a family. For us, participation in a team sport was important and our children didn't have that opportunity at school.

Priorities.

When your boss asks you to give him a plan of what you are going to do next month, it's a way for your boss to see if you are organized and potentially productive. Can you do the same thing with your personal life? Can you see in advance that you have to be at your daughter's dance recital or judo competition? Your son's class has a theatrical production at school – mid-week – and he desperately wants you to be there so that you can see him be a singing rain cloud. Can you be there? How much courage does it take to ask your boss if that's okay?

Actually, unless you have a saint for a boss, it takes a lot of courage. How many of us actually negotiated life's little priorities into our work contract… not many, I suspect. What I am trying to say is that we all have to set an example. Don't take advantage of your boss or your time away from the office. If your boss refuses to let you go, cope. Send your spouse with the video camera. In a few years the school will probably have a web cam (if they don't already!) and you can watch it live without ever leaving your office. However, if a lower ranking team member or your personal assistant asks the same thing, don't be your boss. Make the decision that you think is just and fair...put yourself in the other person's shoes.

The bosses of this world were formed by their bosses. They fully believe that they have certain standards to maintain (of course, these standards were originally formed by reading Charles Dickens and they never finished the book to find out that Scrooge was reformed at the end). If we are going to put new priorities in place in the 21st century, we have to be patient.

Just try to focus on the time when your boss will retire, and you (hopefully) will be selected to take his place, and when you get there you will judiciously allow your employees to go home early (with their laptops and high speed internet connections) to see <u>their</u> kids be singing rain clouds. You see, some choices mean putting the priorities on creating happy, productive employees, too.

Okay, I think you see where I'm going with this discussion about daily life priorities. I do have one last word to say on the subject. Do you and your significant other both know how to cook? Do you both know how to do dishes and clean up the kitchen? Do you both know how to do the grocery shopping and run the washer and dryer? Good. That's an excellent answer. There's nothing more irritating to one partner (most notably, the wife) than to be expected to come home every night after work and cook dinner and clean up and do all the laundry.

We are no longer in a one-income world; we haven't been for quite some time. Everyone has to work, but not everyone has to cook dinner every night.... (Was that clear enough?)

Priorities also mean understanding other people's priorities. Learning to share the workload is a good start to a relationship.

Family Life

Are you old enough to remember the television program "Leave it to Beaver?" What a great show…it proved to everyone that Beaver's dad was better than our own because he miraculously came home at 5:00 p.m. and had the time to sit down and read his evening newspaper AND solve all the problems of the world before dinner. The Cleaver family set the tone for the baby boomers about what life should be. Too bad that it wasn't really like that. By the time my father moved into the executive wing, he was out of town three out of five nights a week and home late the other two. I have a few friends who were jealous that my father was out of town because theirs were not, and when they came home they were tired and cranky and yelled a lot.

I'm very impressed that my very modern sister-in-law who works for a big management consulting company negotiated Fridays at home to be with her two small children. That's very European thinking. I was even more impressed when my spouse left the hotel management job he held proudly – even defiantly – for 10 years to be at home more with our kids. Okay, so he had a mid-life crisis when he made this decision. He recovered! He teaches English as a second language and is home every night for dinner and never works weekends. He did this for his kids and for the family equilibrium. It was a family life priority. It took a lot of courage to do and 2 years of not making much money at all. He's not alone in making this kind of decision.

"When my two daughters were little, 4 and 6, my wife decided that she didn't really want to be a wife or a full-time mother any more. We ended up getting divorced and the girls stayed with me. There were tough times but I have no regrets. I got my girls through adolescence, college and young adulthood. Now they are both moms and they are both doing great jobs and both working full time. When they were little, we got through the difficult times because we had a level of trust and respect between us. Yes, I had to make some decisions about my own personal life, and my work, but it had always been clear that my number 1 priorities were my girls. I made a home for them… a home that they could be proud of and happy in. I didn't run home to my parents for help. I didn't marry someone to support me. I did it on my own. I managed my job as well as house, home, and children, and I stayed in the same town so that the girls could continue to see their mother. Yep, a lot of times I put their needs before my own… and I would do it all over again the same way if I had to."

Thomas
Colorado, USA

If you have family, you are constantly faced with choices. Who is going to take care of the parents when they can't take care of themselves? Who will pay for the private school that costs more per year than our four years of university combined? Is summer camp for two weeks an option this year? Is a better or larger car a possibility? With an unstable economy, can we take the risk to buy a new home or just stay in the small apartment that we already own? Choices and more choices.... Answers come from finding the priorities.

You don't have to be married with children to have family choices. If you are single and gay, do you go home for the end of the year holidays and face your family who can't cope with your lifestyle choices? If you just got divorced, how do you cope with not seeing your kids at Christmas just because this isn't your year? The list of examples is endless – in a modern world there is so much outside influence on our lives that the choices needing to be made seem to go on forever. But these choices must be made – by trying your best with your own resources to put things into perspective and by choosing your priorities.

If you are the one who has the kids this year for Christmas, remember that your "ex" doesn't. Try to find some special time for them to be with the other parent. Don't be selfish. If you are single and gay (or single and not gay) and you don't want to go home for the holidays, but it's better than being alone, think, "Hey, maybe I won't be alone next year and they *ARE* family."

"I grew up without siblings. My friends were my priority. I drove my parents crazy because

whenever I came home from college all I wanted to do was see my friends – they replaced the brothers and sisters I didn't have, but my parents never understood that. In contrast, my parents' priority was for me to be home with them. As you can imagine, this created tension. Hindsight, however, has not changed my attitude. My friends were my priority in my life. Now my priorities have evolved, but my friends are still very important to me. My husband has his brothers and sister; I have some very close friends, and now I really enjoy just going 'home'."

Liz
Connecticut, USA

What's important is that you can see where the priorities are in your life as you live it today.

"My family's priorities evolved significantly when we found out my wife was expecting our first child. I was unemployed and my wife was working as a consultant. Nothing stable. Not a great situation. We had been calling into question many things about work and what was important in our lives when we received the news, and it sort of jolted us into reality. I had grown up in Europe and didn't like the way people were so attached to their jobs in the U.S. We started talking about what life was like for me growing up in France, and we decided to move "back home." My mother tried to warn me that this was going to be a huge shock for my wife…she was right. Not only was moving to France a cultural shock but so was being at home with a

small baby. I was suddenly working what seemed like unending hours (my idealistic memories of France in the 1960s were not the reality of France in the 1990s...), and my wife was home with a newborn baby. She missed her work life and the intellectual stimulation. We went through some very difficult times but we got through it. We have learned to be adaptable..."

Patrick
Versailles, France

Nothing prepares people for being a full-time parent. You are no longer THE priority and there's no going back. The first few years are difficult, but in many European countries woman have choices. It's not socially unacceptable to stay home with your children. As a matter of fact in many Scandinavian and European countries, France for example, you can take a leave of absence from your career to raise your children and come back and step in where you left off. You don't necessarily have the same job description as before, but you return at the same job level as before. You decide the time you are going to take off: 3 months, 6 months – 6 years...

"I went back to work 10 years after I had my first child. I had a few short-term, part-time jobs during those years, but I feel that I was present with my children when they needed me and I thoroughly enjoyed being able to be there with them. It wasn't always rosy – many times I envied my friends who kept working, but many of them envied me much more. When I returned to work, it was at full speed. By December of that year, I realized that the children still needed me (a little

bit), so I reduced my hours to have more time for them. I also realized that I wasn't super mom. I couldn't juggle a full-time job, manage the household, and give proper attention to the children all by myself. The flextime at work gave me the opportunity to make my children the priority in my life and still have a job that I enjoyed.

"During those years I realized how much working needed to be a priority in my life again: seeing and speaking with other adults (and not about each other's children!), using both sides of my brain, and being considered as something other than just my children's mom."

Sonia
Noisy le Roi, France

Not everyone has this kind of opportunity. For Sonia, it was unique experience. She thoroughly enjoyed herself, and it gave her the chance to look at what her job priorities were.

When my own children were little, I certainly didn't want to work full time if I didn't have too – not as long as the kids were still in elementary school. I was fairly certain that I never wanted to see the inside of an advertising agency again – at least not a big one. I sort of thought that I would like to work for a non-profit agency – one that supported a cause that I believed in; one that might need some new publicity ideas. On the other hand, if I was going to give up my mom status, I wanted to start bringing in money to the family bank account again….

It came down to my family life priorities. When the kids were still young, I found a job that meant I could take them to school and pick them up in the afternoon (there aren't yellow, door-to-door school buses in France… as a matter of fact, it's the parents or nothing…). I had one day for myself and one half day for appointments with reading therapists and doctors for the kids. I had to be really organized with my time but it functioned pretty well…and a lot of laundry got done on the weekends and on my "day off."

I repeat that this is a unique situation. To be able to sit back and decide what you would like to do when you grow up (once you're already grown up) is very special and – to a certain extent – delicate. It's not the kind of thing you can do twice in a lifetime. You have to have the courage to decide truthfully with yourself what your strong points and weak points are, what you want to do with them, and then find the job that fits your priorities in your life. Sometimes it means getting paid less money. Can you afford to do that? Sometimes it means moving your family – will they cope with that decision as well as you? Does your job decision also affect your spouse's job? Having priorities in your life is good – having good lines of communication between all members of your family is equally important. You can't put together family priorities if you don't have all the information.

From where I sit, things seem pretty clear most of the time. I try to sort through all the information that comes through our lives every day, and we make decisions based on the priorities of our family. When I started writing this book, our oldest son was 12. That was 12 years after we made a calculated decision to move to France to seek a better life for our family. Had we succeeded? I think so. From a quality-of-life standpoint, I believe so. France, and many of the European countries, has 5 weeks of vacation as a starting point. Yes, that leaves some top executives with 10 to 12 weeks of vacation per year – which they generally can't take -- but with 5 to 6 weeks per year you really feel that you have the time to spend with your family and relax.

> *"We like traveling and visiting other countries. In order to have vacation time – as a family – we 'share' the small school vacations. One of us takes the kids during October vacation, the other takes them skiing during February vacation, and then we alternate again for April vacation. It's not ideal, but this way we don't use up all our vacation time. We are all together for the long Christmas vacation and three weeks in the summer. We travel and take the kids places so they are exposed to other cultures and ways of life."*

> Paul
> Caen, France

What gets lost in the push and shove? There is often little time for the "couple." Mom and Dad are no longer Husband and Wife until the kids are much older. It's tough. You have to keep reminding yourselves that for 10 to 15 years – or longer – of your communal life that your children are your priorities. It's difficult on the emotional plan too. Those children are very demanding: 24 hours a day demanding. If one of your single friends makes fun of you for opting to stay at home with the kids for a few years, suggest that he or she trade places for a week or so. Seriously. That usually ends the discussion.

Once our kids were old enough, I went back to work full time. Guess who took up the slack when I was travelling? My husband. Remember what I said about both parents being able to cook, clean, and do laundry? He didn't like it, but he was often 'Mr. Mom' when I would go on business trips for a week at a time or more... Our kids survived and it showed them that a women's place can be shared between home and the office. This *IS* a priority for young women today as our social standards are finally starting to shift toward more balance and equality. I'm not saying that stay-at-home parents are not socially correct. I'm suggesting that it doesn't always have to be the mom...

Women have traditionally and socially been expected to 'keep house'. Thankfully this is changing but it has taken a long, long time. People who have never been faced with the situation do not realize that being at home is a full time job. Being a stay-at-home parent often means giving up the housekeeper, the dog walker, and generally a lot of luxuries. When your teenagers grow up, push them to do internships in everything they are interested in, but also encourage them to take one summer off and be a nanny or an au pair girl or boy. I did it one summer and it changed my life. (As my husband pointed out, he did his required French military service and I was a summer nanny...what a reality check!) It's a great way to figure out what household and child responsibilities are all about (and get paid for it).

"One year when our kids were little, I took two weeks off from work after the end of the year holidays to get caught up with 'stuff' at home: the laundry, the bills and general paperwork, clothes that needed mending, costumes that needed to be made for school, cleaning out the closets, organizing who needed what in terms of school clothes, the minor operation that one of the dogs needed, a doctor that I had been waiting to see for a few months but hadn't had time...the list goes on and on. I was more tired at the end of those two weeks than when I was working full-time because, besides all those things, I still had to do the grocery shopping, the cooking, getting the kids to and from school, to their tennis and pony lessons on time, and just as I thought I was getting caught up, the littlest one came down sick with the flu... 4 days lost."

Anne-Lynn
Massachusetts, USA

Time seems to pass slowly as we are living it but if you look behind you, you will realize just how quickly it has actually passed. The children will not be little for very long. Yes, this period of our lives seems interminable because there is such a concentrated effort focused on the raising of "the child", but when it comes right down to it, the children grow up pretty quickly. They also are much more self-sufficient than we were at their ages... Answering machines, cell phones, and the internet have made their world smaller and to a certain extent more controllable. Although with the extended freedom remains a minimal dependence on the parents. The kids know where they are supposed to be when – but they also know exactly when you are supposed to be there to pick them up again.

> "*When our girls were little we had them in after-school programs. When they say last pick-up at 6:00 pm., they mean LAST pick-up. They charged $2.00 for every minute you were late PER CHILD. I had a list of all my friends and their cell phone numbers on the sun screen of my car. When you get stuck in California rush-our traffic, there isn't much you can do but seek help from a friend. My friends would just let the girls and their kids play in the playground until I got there...*"

> Anne
> California, USA

Children today generally cope better with parents who have been delayed because there is a communications link established with the parents or caregivers. They know they have not been forgotten; they receive instructions and have learned to wait.

I'm sure that you have situations in your life all the time in which you have to decide between two or more options. You can't do everything, and some things are more important than others. You do your best to make the best decision; you look at the options presented to you and decide, rationally, which one is more important – maybe you'll regret the decision later, but you'll learn from that experience.

There is a wonderful line in the beginning of the movie "Hook[1]" starring Robin Williams as Peter Pan. He and his family are visiting "Granny Wendy" in London and he is negotiating a big business deal on his cell phone and not paying attention to what's going on around him. Maura, his wife, takes the phone away from him and throws it out the window and says, "Peter, you're missing it. You're missing them grow up. They want to spend time with you now and you're missing it. In a few years they won't want to be with you anymore."

I forced my husband to listen to that. It's a truth; a truth to be paid attention to…and sometimes it's the truths in our lives that define what we consider to be our priorities.

You can see in your own lives where you have options and which ones you can and cannot take advantage of. Those are your priorities as they are presented to you. But remember that it's through communication among all the members of your family that you define what your family's priorities are. If there aren't strong lines of communications, then it won't work right. You need to maintain a constant understanding with your spouse/significant other about what the priorities are. If one of you goes through a rough period for a couple of months, then perhaps you need to make an adjustment in the priorities – he or she might need help or just some time off. Or perhaps you do need to take a very long weekend just for the two of you…to remember who you are…to remind yourselves that you were the start of this

---

[1] Hook produced by Steven Spielberg, starring Robin Williams and Dustin Hoffman.

family. Plan in advance, get the kids invited to friends' for the weekend or ask someone to come in and take care of them, but take the time necessary for you as a couple.

One thing that many people forget is that maintaining the family as a whole unit is a priority for everyone – not just for the couple or for the children. If you can avoid a separation through better communication, then COMMUNICATE.

> "*Looking back, our friends always thought we were the 'perfect couple'. After our second child was born, things started falling apart between the two of us. My husband's a great father; I think I'm a great mother. Together we are great parents, but we no longer formed a great couple. I realize now that we had stopped talking to each other about us. Our only concerns were the children and our jobs. We love the kids, but we forgot to love each other. Over time – several years – the lines of communication got worse and worse. First I moved into another bedroom then made the decision to move with the children to an apartment not too far away. At no time did we ever speak to each other nor seek assistance from someone. After about 4 months I began to realize that perhaps this was not the decision to make. I didn't want to lose what I had with this man. My friends suggested that we try talking to a counselor and try to work things out. There's a lot of hurt that needs to be healed and forgiven. The four of us make a*

great family, but, if the couple doesn't function the family doesn't either."

Jenny
Illinois, USA

Communication is the key to everything in a family, and you cannot define the family priorities if you don't have all the information.

Divorce, unhappily, does happen. People do realize that they are just not meant to live together. When that does happen, and if there are young children involved, please be adult about it – that is what you are: adult. Don't use the children against the other spouse and remember that you love those children even if you don't find the love you had for the other parent.

> *"One of my best buddies from primary school was suddenly faced with the divorce of his parents. I think we were maybe 10 years old at the time. The parents simply said that the mother didn't want to live with his father anymore. They handled the split as well as they could and tried not to involve the children in their own separation. At first, the kids spent equal time with both parents. They switched from one apartment to another in the middle of the week and spent every other weekend with the other parent. As time went on, as his mom got on with her new life, she became more distant and the kids spent more time with their dad. Both kids had learning disabilities and they suffered not having their parents as one unit supporting them.*

Watching what happened to my friends made me realize that my family wasn't perfect but my parents supported me 100 percent. I get it. Divorce happens... but what that taught me is to always make my kids my priority, no matter what. We have to be there for the kids to help them grow up."

Chris
Versailles, France

So, the conclusion to this is simple. Family priorities can only be found through communication from all the family members. Everyone's feelings, needs, and desires must be taken into consideration. For what seems like endless years, the parents *need* to put the children first as much as possible but still remembering who they are: two parents who founded a family; two parents who love each other.

Raising Children

One of the flaws in the whole child raising process is that children don't come with an instruction guidebook. There are tons and tons of books out there on how to raise children but which ones are good and which ones are old fashioned?

What little knowledge we do have comes from how we were raised. Some of us were lucky and some of us were not so lucky. And now, assuming that you have decided to start a family with your significant other, there are two of you with two different opinions.

I am not going to sit here on a throne and pontificate on how to raise children. I came with baggage that many years with a psychologist helped me change, but not after being too rough on my first two children. My father wanted me to have a better life than he did and, unfortunately, when I wasn't living up to his expectations, he punished me the way he was punished, by smacking and spanking me, and when I got older by belittling me and telling me I wouldn't amount to anything.

I think he realized along the way that he had repeated his own father's behavior and he tried to make amends. I have done the same with my kids. I find myself apologizing a lot...

Unfortunately, raising children is trial and error. It's also about watching how your friends are raising their children. What can you learn from them - both the good and the bad?

> *"My father never, ever reprimanded us in public. It wasn't 'British'. When my brother and I misbehaved, my father would calmly say, 'David, could you come see me outside?' He rarely raised his voice but it was made clear to us that what we had done was not proper... and it was always done in private; just him and me.*
>
> *"Yes, we occasionally were spanked when we had done something wrong repeatedly (torturing the nanny, for example, which was one of our favorite 'sports' when we were about 8 and 10 respectively), but it was rare... When we got older and would visit our father in his London law office, we occasionally heard him say to a young associate, 'Could I see you in private for a moment?' and we knew the guy was in trouble!"*
>
> David
> London, UK

I was at a horse competition in France a few years back and saw a dad give his son a quick smack on the back of the head. I couldn't say anything to him but I realized it was how his father had probably treated him.

Yelling, screaming, throwing pots and pans, hitting... It's a learned reflex that is hard to unlearn. Hypnotism is a good quick fix but it doesn't take away the gut instinct that was ingrained in us by our parents. That takes time to learn to forgive.

It's a primal instinct to defend oneself. Our society says to not harm others yet all you see on the news, in TV series and in the movies is people – even kids – killing others or blowing up groups of innocent people.

How can we stop this scenario? We are our children's role model. We have to do our best to guide them along their way and teach them from an early stage what is correct. It we punish them for doing something by yelling or hitting, they learn this is okay.

Two wrongs don't make a right...

"My sister had a nasty temper when we were children. She was always the one pulling someone's hair at school or poking someone from behind. She was even more obnoxious with me, her little sister. I can't say that her temper improved with adulthood; she was always quick to respond. When she started having her own children, my siblings and I all agreed that it would be an 'amusing adjustment' for her. In fact, she learned the 'time out' technique from a close college friend and she applied it fairly. I arrived one weekend and was greeted at the door by my 6 year old nephew. He gave me a big hug and whispered in my ear, 'Mommy can't come see you right now. She's on a time-out'. And there,

sitting on the bottom rung of the staircase, was my older sister who had given herself a time-out because she had yelled at the kids for making too much noise unfairly."

Mandy
Texas, USA

What do we want for our children? We want them to be happy, mentally healthy adults. To do that we need to set examples. Choose the company you keep wisely and your care-givers!

"*When we had our first child I went back to my part-time job after 2 months. We had the most wonderful au pair girl. Our second child was born 16 months later and by that time we had a new au pair. I can't describe how horrible this girl was. We sent her packing after 3 months – the time it took us to figure out that she was ignoring the babies most of the day and talking on the telephone with her boyfriend long-distance. This was before 'nanny cams' so we never knew what went on but he was afraid to sleep in the dark for a long, long time…*"

Ella
Oslo, Sweden

If you have issues with the way a buddy behaves, make decisions. Ask him (or her) to clean up their behavior. If they don't, what's more important? A slightly weird friend or your children?

"*We have cut off people from our 'friends list' because they were setting the absolutely wrong example for our kids. We miss some of them and wonder how they are faring, but we have no regrets. Kids need to see from a very young age what is acceptable behavior, that learning is hard work, and that growing up is not an optional activity.*"

James
Massachusetts, USA

"*My mother always had interesting friends. It wasn't until I was much older that she admitted that a lot of them were there to ensure I was surrounded by amazing women. The most remarkable was my 'Aunt Clare'. She taught me so much that I could write a book about her. She taught me to always offer the guy working at the house a coffee, a sandwich or a beer; to take the time to let them know they were appreciated. She was also my cushion when my mom was being too strict. She would calmly explain why. She wasn't my mom so there was less conflict, I could talk to her about almost anything, and I had the upmost respect for her. When she died suddenly I was devastated. I just thought she would always be there for me. Now I try to live up to the image she had of me.*"

Liz
Maine, USA

We are allowed to make mistakes; to do otherwise would be impossible. Another important thing is to say you are wrong when you've made a mistake and to apologize for it. I know. My kids tell me constantly that I'm wrong about things... fine. I'm still learning at my age!

Here's an example: you've had a long day at the office, traffic was horrible on the way home. You are tired and frustrated. Your 5 year old is clinging to you and asking for something repeatedly while you are trying to make dinner. As a reflex you shout at the child, or push her away and she falls. She starts crying... This is where you take a deep breath, turn off the stove, pick her up to sooth her and say you are sorry. Now take a second deep breath and remember this moment so it won't happen again.

Do you understand? Wants and needs come into play in almost every circumstance if you step back to look at the situation and analyze it. Learn from your errors and your parents' or teachers' errors. Develop the good habits, squelch the bad ones. Evolve. That is what we are here for...

You *want* your children to become happy, well-balanced adults. If you *need* to do so, make changes to your lifestyle to ensure this works.

Education

How can you teach your children to make their education their priority? I'm not sure I know – if you have some brilliant idea, please call me. All I can transmit is what I've come across so far and the trauma we experienced…

First of all, remember that we are our children's role models – us and our family and the friends we keep (*See note about weird friends from the last chapter…*). Children learn by watching and listening to the adults around them. If they see that you don't care about your work, then they'll think that it's not important to care about theirs…and their work is learning. Don't hide your problems at work from your children, but be careful what you say and how you say it. They shouldn't get the impression that going to school is an option.

I wish I could say that there is some magic phrase that we should repeat to our children every day to explain that they have to invest themselves at school – but it just doesn't work that way. You can't expect your child to be the best at modeling clay or the Matisse of finger painting. You can't say, "You have to be the first one in your kindergarten class to learn to read." I know. I've been there.

"All three of our children have some sort of learning challenge. Our oldest son has dysgraphia. His first few years at school were like going through hell and back again. It took him two years to learn how to read; he had to go through first grade twice; he had a reading therapist two hours a week for three years plus after-school tutors to help with homework. He finally learned how to read then had to go to someone else to learn how to understand what he read. Torture: for him and for us. And, as if to pour salt on to the wound, his little brother learned to read in three weeks all by himself; and yet the little brother couldn't do math.

"For all three, self-esteem and confidence were low throughout primary school. Even if they didn't understand something immediately, we would remind them of something they did learn easily. We tried to take the time to sit with the kids and explain things. Not always easy since mathematics have changed since we were kids...a lot! Reading programs are different too, although we learned quickly that the best method was and still is learning your letters, then syllables, then words, then sentences.

"My wife can't do math and I hate to write. It repeated in our kids. At least they aren't being treated like idiots or 'slow' like we were in school."

Benjamin
California, USA

Give your kids a place to work when they get older. Even make a big deal out of buying a desk and making a space for it in their room. Get a good lamp, give them the tools they need at each age and make sure they know how to use them. Get a chair with adjustable seat height so they have good posture. If there's room, get a small stool so you can sit next to them when they need help. Make it clear that this is their study space – just like you have a desk at work – and just like your boss expects you to keep your office neat, you expect them to keep this space clean so that they can work properly.

When I first started writing this book, kids still didn't have their own computers or tablets. Now, it's common and the advantages to these kids are enormous. Being able to look up anything on the internet in real time, no more need to hunt through library stacks for research information, spell-check. Kids in the 21st century don't know how easy they have it. Do they abuse this technology? Absolutely YES. We have one TV. It's in the TV room. Does our daughter sit in her room and watch TV on her iPad? YES. Does it irritate us? YES! Have we figured out a way to control her screen time? No... but she does know that homework and school projects get done before play and before the computer games, Facebook, and Instagram go on. Priorities. This is where it starts.

When they are little and get an assignment for a project at home, guide them. Don't do it for them but show them how to organize their work. If you do that with them a couple of times, they'll understand for the future. It's all about building their confidence. Walk them through their first book report. When it's finished, ask them to present it to everyone at dinner one night before it's due in school…and make sure everyone applauds at the end! Do the same thing with assigned poetry. Build their confidence. Don't overdo it. Be fair with them; tell them when it's good and when it needs a little more work. Remind them that you went through this too… If you can accomplish this, half the battles are won. Key points? Organization. Concentration. Looking for the priorities in their work. They shouldn't think they will get a blue ribbon or a gold star for everything they do; only for the projects they do that deserve reward.

Positive influences

> "*I wasn't a bad student but I was lazy. I had the horrible habit of leaving papers and projects until the last minute, and I wasn't a good judge of the time it would take to do something. It was a good thing that I could think at the typewriter, but I did have a tendency to turn things in late (and lose points on the grade)…Until I met Mrs. Sheila Shaw: my freshman English professor. The first day of class she handed out the syllabus and announced that all papers would be turned in on the day requested at the beginning of the class. No late papers would be accepted. Period. I still had a tendency to wait until the last minute to write them …but with Mrs. Shaw they were NEVER late.*"

Caroline
Massachusetts, USA

How do you explain to a small child or an adolescent that it's important to do the best that they can? Build confidence in them when they are little and spend the next 20 years reminding them that they should always try to do their best...and try to trust them. With any luck they will meet someone along the way who will – in another way – reinforce what you told them. For some reason we don't listen to our parents as well as we listen to others. It must be something genetic because everyone I speak to say the same thing. A human fault, perhaps. Yes, it's true that we learn from our mistakes, however painful those mistakes sometimes may be. Hope that they meet that someone special in their lives early.

My special teacher was the girls' varsity basketball coach in high school: Miss Beltz. A wonderful woman full of intelligence and spunk – for want of a better word – who took me aside one day in practice and said that I wasn't making an effort. I answered that this was just a practice and not a game so why push myself? She remained very calm and said to me, "If you don't make an effort to show me what you are capable of in practice, then no one will see what you are capable of in the next game because you'll be warming the bench." I understood what she was saying to me; what my parents had been saying to me...but of course I understood it better coming from someone other than my parents. Be the best you can be all the time. You'll show people what you are capable of and you can always be proud of yourself, which is, of course, what's really important.

Miss Beltz passed away a few years ago. I hope she had the same effect on hundreds of other students who took her classes as she had on me. What would I have done if I hadn't met Miss Beltz? I hope that there would have been others. I hope that there are wonderful people in this world who have helped you and who will help your children. I can equally say that I hope I have helped or will help someone other than my children and that you will be able to do the same.

What's the end result of all the time and effort with my friend Benjamin's oldest son? He's 2 years behind his friends but after a LOT of hard work he is a junior in college. He chose the school he wanted to go to and once he was able to take only the subjects he was good in, he became an honor student.

His parents think he still lacks confidence in himself. College is a daily battle but it's a war that he is winning. He has learned that he's an excellent team member and he selects the teams he works with well. This too has been a boost of confidence for him. Everything that happens is based on his trust in himself, his organization and concentration - and the fact that his parents trust him.

How do you know when your child is in the right school? That's a really tough question. I used to always think that a good student – a motivated student – would do well anywhere. I'm sorry to say that it's just not true and sometimes parents have to make a judgment call and change schools. Sometimes it means looking seriously at the family's finances to see whether you can afford a different, possibly more expensive, school. Sometimes you can and sometimes you can't. If you can't change, get tutors – hire a high school student or a retired teacher to help them. Do whatever it takes. That's called educational priorities. They can be very difficult decisions. The current cost of a good education in the

United States is out of control. The problem is that parents have made priority decisions to put their kids in expensive private schools to guarantee that they get the best education they can... and the costs have just skyrocketed. The high school that I went to in the 1970s was $4,000 a year; my first year college costs were less than that. That same high school now costs more than $45,000 a year, and the college...well, I'm sure you know. I just hope that the teachers are better paid now than they were when I was a kid!

So what do we get out of all of this? Work with your children. Try to guide them, help them. Support them when they need supporting and let them fly solo when you think they are ready. Test them and find out early where their aptitudes are and channel their energies.

Ask your children to do their best and when it's not enough, ask them if they think that they can do better; but accept their answer when they say that they've done their best.

Please teach them early to use a keyboard correctly (not with the two index fingers...) and work with them on the computer, don't just let them discover on their own.

If they do well in school, they will hopefully be able to choose well what they *want* to do when they grow up – and if they choose well, they will be happy at work – and if one is happy at work it's easy to get up in the morning....

Ah! If it were only that easy....

Life's Challenges: Great or Small

Everyone faces challenges in their life. Some are born with them, some acquire them along the way, and other people just have big or little ones that they must face up to every now and then.

The word 'challenge' has been infused with several meanings over the last millennium. In the fourteenth and fifteenth centuries, it was a legal term meaning 'to dispute, accuse', which is left over from the Anglo-French (challenging to a duel, and all that, if one's home, property or honor had been threatened). This still holds true today in legal jargon, though by 1954 a challenge in noun form was also considered 'a difficult task'.[2]

In 1985, to 'be challenged' had become a politically correct euphemism for having a disability of one sort or another, be it physical, mental or - in a wider sense -

---

[2] http://www.etymonline.com/index.php?allowed_in_frame=0&search=Challenge&searchmode=none

social or family related. A challenge is something that tests you, whether you are being judged against the abilities of others, or just testing your own strengths.

There is no 1-to-10 scale reflecting how difficult one person's challenges are compared to those of another person. The 'challenge' is how well you step up to face your own situation.

There are many who believe that we choose the life we are living; that, before we are born, our souls make a judgment of the situation and decide if they can handle what is being set before them in the physical world. This would mean that we are prepared to face the challenges in our lives that we have chosen to take on.

Others believe that nothing happens without a reason. Personally, I do not believe that we are being punished when something bad happens to us or to the people around us. Taking on difficult tasks or challenges are a means for growth. We strengthen our souls by accepting challenges!

Do you have challenges in your life? I do! Some are physical (small), one is mental (medium), and one is social (it's small, a 1 on a scale of 1-10 for me, but seen very differently by my entourage).

I'll tell mine...

Physically, I have one challenge that was short-lived but left lifelong effects. I woke up one morning in college with an enormous 'zit' on my face. The next day there were two... And then it got worse. It turned out to be some sort of hormonally-based acne, but it was almost a year before the doctors got it under control, and my face was scarred for life. I've had two surgeries to try and reduce the scarring but I have a face that is clearly marked. Try singing in the college choir or taking public speaking classes when you have terrible swollen marks on your face. All I wanted to do was shut myself in a closet and hope they would go away but I couldn't. I blocked out the image that I saw every morning in the mirror and went on with my life. People stared at me, some people told me how sorry they were for me... I got through it. I became tougher. I got rid of most of the mirrors in my apartment. Finally, the marks went away but not without leaving physical and emotional scars.

My mental challenge is dyscalculia - a learning challenge that impacts mathematical ability. Beyond basic arithmetic, I'm lost. The moment numbers and letters are mixed, my brain shuts down. I live better in a metric world than an Imperial one because the metric system is more straight-forward and logical. I have never known what X equaled. I can do spread sheets and balance my budget at work but it stops there. It kept me out of higher science classes at school and university. I wanted to study architecture but couldn't pass the math requirements. Dyscalculia presented an impassable obstacle that deterred me from pursuing a career in one direction.

My social challenge is my personality. I am highly intuitive but I'm also horribly dogmatic. I'm difficult to live with. I say what I believe, sometimes quite too loudly and freely...often without giving the situation in which I'm speaking quite enough consideration. This has cost me my job in a few situations and I have spent my entire life trying to situate myself better in society. My husband is a saint for putting up with me. I've always wondered if I didn't fall somewhere in the low end of Asperger's scale... I laugh it off and say, "I'm not that smart; I'm just difficult." At my last job they said I was brilliant, but crazy. Society's penchant for qualifying extends to naming what is not entirely grasped. At work, because they didn't know how to deal with me on a normal level, they named me crazy.

My challenges are nothing compared to those of many people but they are *my* challenges. They have taught me to be less judgmental of others and they have given me the gift of the deepest empathy. I have been stared at because of a disfiguring skin disease. I don't stare at other people because they are different. Everyone has challenges whether you can see them or not.

Says Brent E. Betit, Ed.D., who oversees the Academic and Training division at the Prince Salman Center for Disability Research in Riyadh:

"Differences should not divide us. True respect for diversity should extend to every aspect of our life situation - and should bring us together as singular members of humanity united - not divided - by our differences."

Dr. Betit was a staff founder of Landmark College, the world's first college for students with learning disabilities, where he served for more than three decades. He knows what students go through and how demoralizing it is when people call them different.

Our society is extremely judgmental. We must be compared every day to something called 'normal'.

The reality is <u>there is no 'normal'</u> and there shouldn't be any 'different'...but there is.

What *does* it mean to be different?

My challenges make me different but they are my minor challenges. All three of my kids have some form of learning 'dys'function, and as mentioned already, one of my sons was born with a serious heart defect. I have raised all three of them to look beyond their personal challenges and be the extraordinary person they came into this world to be.

If you are missing an arm or a leg, either from an accident or from birth, you have a challenge...but it is only a challenges as compared to what society says is 'normal.'

If you have fallen into the relatively new category of A.D.D. / A.D.H.D. (Attention Deficit Disorder / Attention Deficit Hyperactive Disorder) then you benefit from knowledge and education that many of us did not have. Those of us who have these issues were very poorly treated as children. We were lazy, slow, stupid; (I was a math idiot). Based on research into how the brain functions, there are now teachers and special schools available to help you learn to learn YOUR way and not in the 'normal' way.

If you or one of your children has Down's Syndrome or fall into the autism 'Spectrum', this does not mean that you or they can't function in the modern world. It just means that adjustments need to be made to accommodate you at work or at school. What professors have learned is that people on the Autism 'Spectrum' generally have talents that make them superior at certain tasks than 'normal' people, often due to their ability to hyper focus on their favorite or preferred subjects. Okay, there are social adaptation issues as well, but once again we are comparing to a social norm that enlightened people understand is flawed.

Asperger's Disorder is the perfect example: often brilliant people, just as often completely lacking social clues.

In fact, perhaps we should say that if we have some 'issue' (another lovely euphemism for a 'handicap' or 'disability') we all have social challenges? It is 'society' that judges us as 'different' and 'not normal' because society has decided what normal should be. Oh, by the way, this is known as 'social injustice'.

Take the example of people who have family challenges. First let's consider what is a 'family challenge'? I used to think that a family challenge was a sociological or educational difference. One could be born into a family and not fit in because of a high or low intelligence. Moving outside of that nuclear family situation or being stuck in it could be considered a handicap, or a disadvantage.

One of the top schools in France, l'Ecole Polytechnic, is a military school similar to Massachusetts Institute of Technology. This major French university is very comparable to an exclusive, private club. You get in because you are brilliant but often also because your father or grandfather was also brilliant and attended that university. And once you're in - and you graduate - you are secure for life; you will be hired and protected by other Polytechnicians. It is a self-perpetuating, continuously-reinforcing legacy system.

A few years back, the university started admitting a small percentage of students from areas that were considered 'difficult, challenged, or under-privileged.' For these young people, it was a chance to change their 'family' situation based on what society considered normal.

I'm trying to be as politically correct as I can as I'm writing this. I believe that everyone comes into this world as equals. What happens from there is based on educational, economic, or social advantages or disadvantages. This is not to say that being from a well-educated, or moneyed family is an advantage!! You have but to read social magazines or watch reality TV to see that young people who have been brought up with wealth are not necessarily the brightest lights on this earth, nor are they the most socially responsible. Given the destructive outcomes of so many of these privileged young people, we might conclude that wealth presents its own handicap.

For many *MANY* years I've wanted to write a book entitled "There's No Such Thing as a Non-dysfunctional

Family." (I still may... Give me time to finish this book first.) I simply cannot think of one family in my large entourage that is 'normal'. Everyone has a challenge to overcome, whether it's physical, mental, social, or family. EVERYONE has had to overcome SOMETHING!

But once again, this brings us back to what is 'normal!'

Two more quick paragraphs on mental challenges: do you or someone you know have a 'mental challenge' based on chemical imbalances? I'm referring to mental disorders such as bi-polar, depression, schizophrenia, and the like. Well, my family does. Not in our nuclear family but in our close group of friends.

Similar to how a slow or lazy student is now diagnosed with A.D.D., many of these conditions – which have always been there – have new names because medical science has been working to better identify and help people with these conditions. If your doctor has suggested and prescribed medications that can help, please take them. Ask a family member or a close friend to be your support team and ensure that you take your meds. These pills will not alter your lifestyle; they will help you enjoy it! I'm not suggesting that you will become 'normal' either because, as stated before, I don't believe there is a 'normal'.

So here's the bottom line....

There is no 'normal.' It's society that has issues, not YOU. Your role while on the earth in this lifetime is do the best you can with what you've been given. Your challenge is to be the best 'you' that you can be.

Don't be judgmental about other people. You don't know what their challenges are. Teach your children not to stare at individuals who aren't the same as you or them. Explain to them that everyone IS different and it's these differences that make us each unique and makes the world more interesting. Dr. Victor E. Frankl, a neurologist, psychiatrist, holocaust survivor, and author said, "*The way in which a man accepts his fate and all the suffering it entails, the way in which he takes up his cross, gives him ample opportunity – even under the most difficult circumstances to add a deeper meaning to his life.*"

Remember: there is NO NORMAL. You are unique! You don't want to be simply 'normal.' It is your uniqueness that differentiates you from everyone else and that makes you both special and an individual!

Accept your challenges. Be special. Succeed at being you and you will live a happy life!

Money

The American consumer was brought up on the idea that anybody could have anything as long as they worked hard and had a good credit rating. Well, it seems that the best way to get a good credit rating is to have one credit card that you use one time and pay off in three monthly installments and never use again unless it's an emergency. I believe that the first decade of the 21st century taught people all over the world something important: Don't use credit. Don't spend what you don't have. Credit should only be used to finance your home, perhaps a new car, or in an emergency… Use debit cards and don't abuse your bank. If you get into a habit when you are young of buying on credit you'll only regret it later. If you don't learn in your youth the value of hard earned money, you probably never will.

Don't give your children allowance money unless it's attached to certain household chores. If you can afford to have household help, find a way to give your children some tasks for which they can be responsible. Even if it's distributing the mail within the house or watering the plants! If they want something – a toy or a new CD – don't just buy it for them: let them earn it. Let them clean out and vacuum the car; let them empty all the wastepaper baskets in the house twice a week. Make someone responsible for setting the table and clearing it off before and after each meal. And don't over pay them! Make them realize what the value of their work is worth. And please, don't pay them for their good grades…what are you going to do, make them pay you back for bad grades?

> *"There have been so many jokes about the difference between new and old money. You can spot new money from a distance because they drive flashy expensive cars, overdress, have spoiled rotten children, and usually live in McMansions. Old money, on the other hand, still have the money because they don't spend it. When I was young, there was a man on our street who seemed poor. It was only after he died that we learned he was a wealthy philanthropist. He lived a happy, frugal life, and he wanted for nothing. He even cut his own front lawn with an old manual push lawnmower!"*
>
> James
> Massachusetts, USA

Up until the boom years of the 1990s, the grocery stores, fast food restaurants, and ice cream shops were filled in the afternoons and weekends with high school kids who needed to earn money to buy an old car to get around in. Once they bought the car, they needed to earn gas and insurance money. Suddenly, kids had everything placed in front of them. Their parents were buying them cars to drive to school, giving them gas money, and paying for their insurance, so the kids didn't need to work.

> *"My parents were fair with me. Yes, I drove to high school in the late '70s...in the old family car (a 1965 Oldsmobile!) and they paid for the gas — just enough to get me back and forth to school. During vacations I worked to earn money to pay for the rest. The only bend in the rule was if I had an internship. One summer I worked writing the news at a local radio station, another at a magazine, another at the local newspaper. I wasn't making a penny, but I was learning something that I couldn't get at school so they gave me survival money. Evenings and weekends I babysat to make up the rest."*
>
> Susie
> Illinois, USA

If your older kids go away to college, get them a family bank card that they can use for emergencies, but make sure the bills come home to you. Don't let them think that they can just charge things and not have to 'fess-up to it.

Remember the story about my giant teddy bear. I bought him on credit and it was a mistake — a big mistake but I keep him to remind me of it.

I grew up with a different household attitude about money than most kids. I had a lot of friends who were simply handed $50 a month (Yes, $50 – even back in the 1970s). Their parents hoped that it would teach them to manage their money. The first couple of months they ran out and spent it all on records and candy and cheap jewelry. Then they had nothing left for school lunches or movies on weekends. I remember one friend who was sneaking peanut butter and jelly sandwiches out of the house for 3 weeks because she didn't have a dime left for lunch at school. I'm sure her mother knew it but let her suffer and learn her lesson.

> *"I was just out of college. I wasn't making very much money, and I was living at a friend's house to avoid living at home. One evening I was out with some high school buddies and was whining about how poor I was. An older brother of one of the guys cut me off and said, 'Stop whining. You're not hungry enough.' I was speechless. He was right. I was just being spoiled. His quip remark made me grow up and I never complained again about not having 'enough'."*
>
> Roger
> New York, USA

Young people should be "hungry" for things; to know what it's like to not be able to afford something they want. Kids need to learn at an early age the difference between want and need, and that you just don't buy things to buy them. There should be a reason to buy it. We never refuse the things our kids need, but if they want something and we don't agree, then they have to earn the money on their own. I guess the best 2012-era story is about a certain winter coat that has been very popular in Europe and the USA the past few years (no names please but generally black, fur collar, and down filled). Our daughter, now 15, has been trying to acquire one of these parkas for the past three winters. I've made it very clear to all concerned that there is no way she needs a winter coat costing more than $500. This decree has been respected. She has a nice warm winter parka and it cost what a winter parka should cost. She needed it.

In the same vein, I needed a new computer this year if I wanted to finish this book. My old one was slow, out of date, and the screen didn't function anymore. My husband offered me a new laptop for Christmas. It's all I need; a simple, basic computer. It's not at all what I wanted… but I couldn't afford what I wanted (well, I *could* but it would have pretty much emptied my bank account). Just as my daughter didn't *need* the designer winter parka, I didn't *need* the fancy computer of my dreams.

> *"My husband told me that when he was in his last year of high school. He went away on a ski weekend with his school and his father gave him emergency money. He didn't really figure that his father would ever ask him to return the money so he basically drank it all away over the weekend. Then he lost his train ticket home and had to call and ask them to wire him more money. His explanation of what happened to the emergency money didn't go over too well either… On the other hand, he never pulled that trick on his parents again."*
>
> Candy
> Colorado, USA

We probably all have stories like this. There wasn't necessarily a financial loss but the knowledge gained from the experience has an inestimable value. We all have to learn from our own mistakes, but setting a good example will help the kids see things more clearly. Say, for example, that you want a new home entertainment system. Can you buy it with money that you've saved up or do you have to use credit. What's going to happen if you have a car accident and need to do major repairs or even buy a new car? Are you going to regret using up your credit? Of course. Could you have foreseen this? Yes. The home entertainment center is a luxury while you probably need the car to get to work and get the kids to school and their various activities.

> "*When I was a teenager I was very jealous of my friends whose parents had installed pools in the backyard or bought big powerboats. It seemed like such luxurious things to have. I asked my father why we couldn't have stuff like that if he was such a big shot at work. He said that those things weren't important. We had a nice house and nice cars and went on vacations. Okay, that's fine, I thought, but THEIR fathers can afford the rest, why can't we? My mother answered very simply: We're paying for your private school and they aren't. We want to make sure you get the best education we can afford.*"
>
> Robin
> Connecticut, USA

> "*One year I wasn't working very hard at school and my father threatened to put me back in the giant public high school. I didn't want to go back so I went and asked the school headmaster how much a year the school actually cost because my father refused to pay for me anymore. The*

headmaster was good. He never laughed, he told me straight out what all the charges were. I got the message. I apologized to my parents and I worked harder at school."

Sarah
North Carolina, USA

Don't spend what you don't have. Luxuries are things that you can pay for in cash that don't take away from your daily living expenses. Try to not let money disputes ruin your husband/wife relationship either. Family finance is something that has to be discussed by the family. No, children don't need to know how much the annual household budget is, but they do need to realize that you are not made of money and that spending money is contemplated and not something one takes lightly. Impulse buying is something we all do, but it must be controlled.

Ideally, we should be able to put 10 percent of our salary into savings... Boy, I wish that were really true. It seems that the cost of living is always one step ahead of me. Last year I earned a little more than previous years and we had a few less expenses. We decided to put my extra salary into a money market account. That's what we <u>decided</u> to do... It didn't actually happen because our washer and dryer decided to die within a month of each other. However, we didn't have to buy them on credit.

This chapter has been filled with too many "don'ts" but what is important is what you can DO. Do talk about money with your spouse. Do calculate if you can spend money on something big before you decided to go out and get it. Try not to get caught off guard; it will only destabilize your confidence in each other concerning money. Do make a family budget and stick to it and do save a little for the occasional night or weekend of folly – because sometimes an evening of dinner and dancing with your spouse or a Sunday at an amusement park with your children is worth more than a little bit of savings in the bank!

Try this: every time you see something in a store or while on-line shopping, stop and think. Do you *NEED* it? Or do you just *WANT* it. And then, two even more important questions: Can you live without it? Can you afford it?

Work

There is a reason that we are talking about Work just after Money and Education. How many people do you think have their mid-life crisis based on a job or lifestyle they are no longer happy with? There are no precise figures but I can assure you that it's high.

"Oh my God. What have I done? I've wasted half my life doing a job I don't like." Could that person have foreseen the future? No.

One of my dearest friends – a true to the meaning of "math genius" – went cruising through high school, university, and graduate school and on to a job designing space shuttle engines. It made logical sense to all who knew her. What's she doing now? Restoring stained glass windows, teaching stained glass techniques, and tutoring grad. students in math. Is she happy? Yes, I think so. Is she making the same salary as she was before? No. Family life priority decision. She also has two children and now she can make time to be with them. Do any of our friends remember Maria taking any sort of artistic classes in school? No, she never had time! There was obviously something in her personality that needed to resurface.

The day will perhaps come when she gets a call from the old office that they want her to come back...perhaps. It will be a decision that she has to make. That everyone has to make.

> "*I didn't know what I wanted to be when I grew up. My friends all seemed to be doing what their parents did but I had no interest in my father's line of work. After taking a break from college, I went into the retail business. One of my responsibilities was training the apprentice workers and interns. I lasted not quite 10 years. After my mid-life crisis, I realized that the only things I liked about my job were the client contacts and the teaching. I went back to school and now I teach English as a second language to adults (mostly senior business people). Am I happy? Yes. I like my job, there's almost no stress, and it's easier to get up in the morning if you like what you do.*"
>
> Stephan
> Aachan, Germany

If you are young and reading this, don't wait to have a mid-life crisis to discover that your job isn't everything you wanted. Try to MAKE it everything you want. To do that you have to look at what you do every day and make two lists: what you enjoy and what you don't enjoy. This is not to say that you want to walk into your boss's office and say, "I love doing half my job responsibilities, but I don't want to do the rest." That's called getting yourself fired.

Once you have those lists, study them carefully and make priorities among the things you do. Are there items missing from your list that you would like to do? Are there things that you can do within the confines of your current contract? Or are they things that could be considered extracurricular activities?

When I was working in the advertising agency, my priority was writing...presentations, speeches, programs, slogans, letters, memos, anything, but I also liked doing artistic work and graphics. That job, however, belonged to someone in the art department. It was either go work for a much smaller agency where I could perhaps do a little bit of everything or keep quiet, do my job to the best of my abilities, and seek artistic work elsewhere. I did. I set up a little painting corner in my <u>tiny</u> apartment...I painted, I sketched, and I let out my artistic tendencies for my own benefit on my own time. I worked for me and it helped me relax at home. Later on in my career I realized that my artistic abilities could help me with my Power Point presentations. What goes around comes back around!

Do you see what I'm saying? You don't have to change your job or your job description because you're not fulfilled at work. On the other hand, if there is something on your list that stands out as really painful to you, and you do the rest of your job very well, then you can try to talk to your boss about it. Think carefully about what you are asking. Remember the old adage: Be careful what you wish for, it might come true!

Help yourself, help your children: finding what's right.

How can we guide our children to the right profession? Each child is different. I see our oldest son as some sort of engineer. In third grade he created his own electric board game out of wires, a light bulb and socket, a battery, and a shoebox. Yes, his teacher explained how to do it, but he was finished in 5 minutes and then spent the rest of the time helping his classmates. It was something he instinctively understood. This was also the first time anyone had seen him succeed at something in an academic environment. It was spectacular.

Our second son will probably be literary – time will tell. We will guide them based on their enthusiasm for a subject and what we hope – for them – will be a dream that transforms into reality.

This is from a friend in France who was one of my kids' teachers:

> *"I taught English in a very small private school for children in difficulty—not children with learning disabilities, just difficulties learning—for every sort of reason. There were students there who had been thrown out of the top elitist schools because they were disruptive, kids who couldn't cope with the formal, strict structure of the French national school system. There were a lot of kids with 'learning issues' and some who were simply handicapped. The French school system leaves very little room for individualism, and it simply cannot cope with students with*

learning issues. What will happen to these children when they leave this sheltered world? I don't know. Is there someone who will help them find a career that will suit them, that they can do well, that will fulfill them as adults, so that they will be able to support themselves? There were a handful of students who clearly fell into the 'bright light' category and their parents had put them in this school because they didn't know where else to put them. This was a very complicated place to teach. Channeling the energies of young people is a very difficult task. Trying to help wounded kids find their talent and then find their way… It's what all parents and teachers try to do."

Jennifer
Versailles, France

One thing we did learn with our children along the way is the importance of testing kids early to learn what their aptitudes are. As mentioned before, we have one son who is talented in science, one who has amazing verbal-literary skills. Interestingly, both are very talented in art but in different ways. What we learned is to encourage the work they were doing (and continue to do) in the subjects where they are very strong. We never told them we didn't care about the other grades, but we really pushed them to excel in the subject where we knew they had strengths.

Guiding young people into adulthood is a difficult task for parents and – as we all know – adulthood isn't always something we deal well with ourselves. If seeing a psychologist, psychotherapist, or psychiatrist can help you see your life priorities more clearly, then do it. You don't have to go to the most expensive therapist in the world but you do have to find someone with whom you have a good relationship.

Rabbis, ministers, and priests counsel as well – I got through the death of a very close family friend by talking to a priest. And, I wish to point out, I asked for time off from work from a VERY demanding boss to see the priest a couple of mornings a week for about a month. My boss agreed. He saw that I was suffering and incapable of working at my best. This very learned man was able to remind me about all the good things that I had enjoyed about my friend and that all those memories were still inside me...and they were MY memories. It helped me move on. I'll never forget Gladys; she was one of those women who helped form me as the adult that I am...like the teachers Miss Beltz or Mrs. Shaw or my friend's Aunt Clare who we have spoken about before.

So, what can we get out of this? Get a good education and always do the best you can at something. Be honest and truthful with yourself – it's the only way you can correctly define your life's priorities. If things start getting out of control, at work or at home, don't wait until it's too late: look for help. Don't forget that deep down inside YOU are your number one priority because if you are not happy or not well, you can't help those around you...and that's true for your life at work and at home.

Remember to be truthful with yourself and remember to communicate. Work is a means to an end. We <u>have</u> to work to earn money and we have to have money to survive in 'the modern world'. However, we don't have to be miserable in our jobs.

One last thing about work to the young people just starting out in the working world. When you are at work you are there to do just that: work. You are not there to call your friends at their offices, send emails, or play games. You are not there to find a new boyfriend or girlfriend. If you are sitting in an office, in a store, in a factory, or out on job site you are being paid to be there, not to play or fool around.

One of my first bosses said to me and another young woman, "When you are here between 9 and 5 you are working for <u>ME</u>. I don't care what you do before or after, but when I'm paying you, you work." She was right. Fool around on your own time and somewhere else. Don't abuse the company phone bill. Try not to use your office email for personal messages (because there is most likely an email surveillance system at your office). Be serious at work and you'll advance faster. You can't keep the job that you've sought after if you aren't serious. Let everyone know that when you are at work, work is your priority.

And…. Yes, you *NEED* to work but your job will be more enjoyable if you *WANT* to do it. Educate yourself well and enjoy what you do.

"Mother's Work"

There is one simple hard fact that cannot be overlooked in this world: it's the women who must bring the children into the world. There is nothing that we can do about it. The brave new world created by Aldous Huxley still does not exist. Maybe it's not fair but then think that women have an opportunity that men will never have. Men will never know what it is to have someone growing inside them; they will never be able to give birth – to give life to another human being. Kind of sad when you think about it.

The fact is, however, that in the 21st century women are also now expected to maintain intellectually and financially fulfilling lives as well as being moms. Two very difficult things to do at the same time. Are women capable of doing this? Yes. Are there major sacrifices to be made on their behalf? Yes. What can men do to help? Be there. Be understanding. Don't be childish and <u>don't be selfish</u>.

When your colleague comes running in to a breakfast meeting a little late with what is obviously baby spit on the shoulder of her dark blue suit, don't laugh and say

"Oh how disgusting!" and make fun of her. Instead, unobtrusively readjust her scarf to cover the stain and say something like, "Your daughter left her calling card on your suit jacket..." and smile understandingly. Think about how difficult it must be for your colleague to leave her little baby with someone else all day long...to not be there and see her smile, or see her crawling, or see her take her first steps...

"*I am a graphic artist. When I had my first child I was employed at a nice, small graphics agency with a lot of talented people. When my daughter was born, I took 3 weeks off and was promptly back at work. I was so happy because I had found an excellent daycare situation for my little baby girl. It was just perfect – until about 3 weeks later when, upon picking up my little girl from daycare, the woman said, 'Oh! It was wonderful! Morgan smiled for the first time today!' I was devastated. I missed my daughter's first smile – and she had smiled at someone else. My brain went blank. I picked up my baby and all her belongings told the woman very kindly that Morgan wouldn't be coming back for a while. Once home, I called my boss and asked how important I was to him. Flat out. He said very important. I asked whether it mattered if I was in the office or not? He said no, not really.*

"*That night I set up my drawing board, supplies, and computer at home with a fax. Next to my desk I made a play area for Morgan. From then on I only went to the office for important meetings but worked almost exclusively from home. My daughter was my priority but I also needed to work. I was very lucky because this isn't the case for a lot of moms."*

Melissa

Maryland, USA

I can't count the number of people I know who spend all their extra income on nannies just so that their children are at least at home. In certain circumstances the parents balance their workdays so that one goes to the office very early and comes home early and the other goes in late and comes home late. In many cases the family could survive off of one income, but how well? Would there be sacrifices? Yes, of course. Not all companies understand maternity leaves that last more than six weeks. We even know a family doctor who couldn't take off more than a month after her second son was born. He was bundled off every morning from one grandmother to the other until he was old enough to go to daycare because they couldn't afford home care. Life goes on. Children grow up and go to school and we get over the guilt because we have priorities in our lives and they dictate that we can't do everything we want. That's life.

However, if we can't do everything we would like, we can at least share in the work. Men should know how to take care of themselves and help with the housekeeping. They should not have to be told that something needs to be done, they should be capable of seeing it and doing it. The dishwasher is full – so empty it. That one is easy. Why is it the mom who has to stay home from work when the kids are sick? It should depend on what each one has on their agenda for the day. Not everyone has family or neighbors who are there to help. I know, I didn't. But life goes on and you catch up on the work you missed.

To the women readers: Do the best you can with the time you've got and remember that it's not easy for the fathers either. If you have the incredibly lucky opportunity to organize your time so that you can be with your children and do your job then you have more than the average parent. Congratulate yourself and enjoy it.

Once all my kids were in school full-time, I checked the box that said I was willing to travel 25 percent of my time. It was tough but we all got used to it. In the end, I was the one who had trouble coping with so much time travelling. Luckily I didn't have to cut back; the economy did it for me! Suddenly everyone except top salespeople and senior management was grounded. Phfew!

For the men readers: Try to be helpful and understanding. Not every woman has the maternal instinct but when they do it's a powerful thing. For many women there is a period in their lives when the children simply come first and the husband often gets left behind. Try to not take it <u>too</u> personally! After all, it's all based on your collective priorities.

Many couples divorce because the men can't cope with the fact that THEY are no longer the priority of the family anymore. They find women who make them feel that they are the priority again. Not very fair, is it?

As I said, communication is important and you cannot define family priorities if you don't have all the information. I just recently heard from a good friend that she and her husband were separating. She said, "He wants my full attention, mentally and sexually. We have two small children and I work. I'm too tired to do it all and I think the kids are the priority... so he's leaving..." When she told me this I didn't know what to say. I still don't. It did make me realize that my own husband is pretty special because we got through those years when the kids were little and we just celebrated our 25th wedding anniversary. We had some rough times (ya, okay, *REALLY* rough times). I know he felt neglected but we got through it.

When 'we' make a collective decision to have children, we go from being a couple to being a family. The priorities change and multiply and our own personal feelings no longer have the same weight as they did before.

When you are a mom and an employee, 8 to 10 hours a day at the office plus another 8-hour day at home equals an 80-hour work week. That's just about what one needs to accomplish everything on an average mom's 'To Do' list. Would you give any of it up right now? Probably not. Does your intimate relationship with your husband suffer a little? Probably yes. Moms are often the first ones out of bed in the morning and very tired at night...and often are awakened at least once by the children during the night. Sleep is a major priority to most moms so that we can be close to 100 percent during the day.

Conclusion? Being a working mom is great and very fulfilling...It is also very tiring. Dads *need* to be as helpful as possible. Both parents *need* to try to find time together but remember who the cute little priorities are...

Courtesy

I grew up in a country where courtesy is common. You are taught to be polite. Full Stop.

When I was 30ish, my husband and I moved to France, a country where courtesy is rare. You can't really appreciate how a little courtesy in your day can be appreciated until you're faced with the opposite.

Our neighbors and people we worked with always commented that we were 'so kind, so thoughtful' because we always said hello, asked how things were going, helped older neighbors bring in their groceries or move boxes, and so forth. Any Anglo-Saxon reading this will say, 'So?', but in France it was rare.

When you walk into a small shop, if the sales woman is on the telephone, she tends to stay on the telephone. Anywhere else in the world the clerk would likely say, 'sorry, have to go. I have a customer in the store.' Well, not in France…

When we moved a little north to Belgium, the level of courtesy rose, not like in the UK or the USA, but better.

The typical Belgian shop keeper or cashier is very polite. The drivers tend to be not so polite (or let's just say, they drive like they have something to prove).

The thing is, courtesy is free. It doesn't cost you time or money so why are people so unwilling to offer it? Do you like it when people are spontaneously pleasant and polite? Do you appreciate it when someone allows you to slip your car into busy traffic? I do!

Why is it so hard to be generally nice? I don't believe that the French are mean people; they're not all like that but why can't everyone be nice to people they don't know? We all have bad days when we are pushed and rushed and get a little tense. They can't be in a bad mood ALL the time, can they?

This goes for the workplace as well. It's better to encourage someone than to discourage. If you work in a positive, inspiring atmosphere, you will thrive and achieve great things.

So this is very simple: be nice. You *want* people to be nice to you so be nice to other people. Courtesy is contagious: pass it on (or pay it forward, as the new custom taking hold around the world states).

What should you remember from this, the shortest chapter?

Courtesy is FREE, so be nice!

Sex

There are three parts to this: Young sex, middle-aged sex, and mature sex. What we are talking about are relationships, but what we need to talk about are responsibilities.

Young sex is what we want our children not to have. Many of us grew up in the aftermath of Woodstock, the 1970s, and the 'sex, drugs and rock n' roll' generation. The simple fact is that the sexually transmitted diseases in those days could be cured by antibiotics/penicillin. That's not true anymore. Now STD's can kill you.

I suppose that the good thing that came out of the late twentieth century is that we can talk to our children about sexual relationships without having to talk about the "birds and the bees." Young people are much more aware. Most kids get sex education at school at a young age and then can ask questions of their parents without dying of embarrassment.

However, the facts, and human nature, have not changed in that teenagers have sex without thinking of the consequences. Peer pressure is a major force in their lives. Raising a young teenage boy to have respect for a girl who says "no" when his hormones are raging out of control is very difficult.

Trying to explain to young people that "sex" and "love" should have some sort of correlation is nearly impossible. Expecting our children to be virgins when they get married is, in most situations, no longer even in the equation. The question is how best to deal with the situation.

> *"In our home, humor works pretty well. When my brother and I were clearly ready to start testing our sexual capabilities, our parents bought condoms by the boxful. We even got them in our Christmas stockings for a few years! However, both mom and dad were VERY clear about one thing: NEVER have unprotected relations. My mom (who could be a bit scary) said, 'If you catch an STD it could kill you; if you bring a girl home pregnant you should worry that I might kill you.' Wow. THAT worked! We are pretty open with them now about our relationships and we joke about it. Our parents try to be 'cool' and we aren't afraid to talk to them. They say it's all part of our continuing education."*
>
> Alex
> Tennessee, USA

Question: What's the best way to deal with sex and teenagers?

Answer: Education. Before your children start "dating" make sure they know the facts. The facts about STD's, the facts about pregnancies; that they have some sort of understanding in their own terms and language about what to expect from a sexual relationship. Young women need to understand that a lot of young men want to have sex without a relationship. Young men need to understand that most young women want to have a relationship without having sex. This isn't true in all cases, but it's true in a lot of cases.

High school is a major trial-and-error period in children's lives. Luckily the majority of them are living at home and parents can keep an eye on them...at the very least see who they are with and what time they are coming home at night!

If they haven't learned a minimal sense of moral behavior before leaving home for college or university, expect to have some sort of trouble. In saying that, I can't count the number of girls I knew at college who were rational, well-behaved adolescents who lashed out at college! The phrase "having a reputation" meant nothing to these young women, and I'm sure their parents were clueless.

> *"Our family was raised catholic. The fact that our brothers were having sex in high school was blindly tolerated by our parents. Looking back, I know it wasn't fair. Both my sister and I got pregnant before we got married. I married the guy I was dating in college and had my daughter who I love dearly and of whom I'm extremely proud. Our marriage, however, ended in divorce.*

My little sister got pregnant in high school and our parents made her keep the baby then give it up for adoption. So hard... Guess who she never forgave? The Catholic Church. She did forgive our parents; and years later her daughter found her and thanked her for giving her a wonderful life. A happy ending to a really tough situation; and all because we weren't taught about sex properly."

Anonymous
USA

After the infamous university years, relationships seem to calm down. Young men grow into their hormones and figure out that most of the women they are dating want to get married. The fear of becoming a husband and/or father calms down many a young man.

Yes, there is a percentage of young men who are seeking the woman of their dreams – the woman who will be the mother of their children. But let's face it, there are more women looking for the man of their dreams than vice versa.

What is worrisome for all parents is having kids who have no respect for themselves and will jump into bed with pretty much anyone. Male or female: it doesn't matter. It usually takes a traumatic experience to shake them out of it. They won't listen to parents, or siblings. Parents can only be vigilant and be there to catch them and help them get themselves back together.

A more common situation is a young woman convincing herself that she has found 'the one' and letting herself get pregnant.

> *"My daughter, who knew better, came home at 16 and informed us that she was pregnant. We were furious! She was ecstatic with joy, which made us even angrier. We did what we had to do. We got her through it. She stayed in school, had the baby; we helped with the cost of childcare so she could finish high school and then attend college. The baby was her responsibility and – of course – the boyfriend disappeared well before the baby was born. I give her credit; she stepped up and did what she had to do. So we became grandparents early; we got over that. Yes, it was embarrassing for us to admit that our daughter was a teenage mother. In the end it was harder for her. She had dreams for herself. Dreams that were crushed because you can't travel the world with your friends with a toddler in tow..."*
>
> Betty
> Ohio, USA

One 'interesting' development has been the invention of the 'sex friend'. Two people who obviously have fun together but don't want or have time for a real relationship. It's recreational, it's safe-sex, it's un-complicated but it doesn't lead to anything. I know a few younger people who admit to getting through university this way. Okay, as long as everyone is in agreement...

So somewhere in the middle twenties to thirties we find our mates, feather our nests and start laying eggs. Lovely analogy?

Next step: middle aged sex. What this means is that we have stepped into the period where we are raising our children; sex is primarily for procreation and we're too tired to think about being romantic. How to kill a relationship! Funny enough, among most of the women I know, their husbands – despite being highly intelligent human beings – cannot cope with this situation. Remember the discussion about a lot of separations taking place because the men were no longer the priority in their wife's life? This is what it often comes down to: sex.

How can I put this anymore delicately? Women have to try to make an effort despite the fact that all they want to do is sleep. Men have to understand that their wives are also mothers and for several years "mother = exhaustion"; otherwise known as "the heart might be in it but the body needs rest." Conclusion: everyone must try to be understanding – this period in your life shall pass.

Men: You want to have a wild weekend away with your wife? YOU organize the babysitter, all the food shopping and the place to go…99 percent of the wives will beat you to the car to get away for the weekend!!!

And lastly: mature sex. It's what we've been waiting for, right? The children have grown up and moved out – or are at least away for the night or weekend – we know all the moves so now it's time to enjoy each other. For many couple, this is what we've been waiting to get back to.

It's based on mutual respect; it's based on the love that we had for each other when we first met; it's based on having matured together and grown together. It's what "making love" is all about... It's remembering how to enjoy just being with the person we selected to share our lives and our emotions. The person we want to share our deepest feelings with...to love that other being.

For many couples, to reach this place in our lives we have to pass through many doors...together. When you are young it is difficult to focus on what life is going to be like when you "grow up." Much of what we've been discussing, thinking about, has been how to put our priorities in place to move to this level of relationship.

In dealing with sexual relationships, all will confirm that mutual respect is the most important element. If you and your partner have the same priorities in your life, you will share that respect and making love will be just that: showing the other person that you can love them just as much as you can let them love you.

What do you need to retain from the Sex chapter? Communication is extremely important; with your children, with your partner and with your spouse. Understanding each other's *needs* and *wants* should come before anything else (and don't forget to protect yourself!!)

Retirement

Do you have mixed emotions concerning this subject? There's a real love/hate relationship attached to the word 'retirement'. It's something you look forward to, plan for, and yet dread.

Are there ways to properly prepare for and deal with your retirement? Yes, I think so. In any event, if you've managed to make it there, half the battle is won! The big question is, can you deal with it graciously knowing that the next step in your life is….ummm, well, much more peaceful?

How people retire really speaks about their inner selves. My mother retired, officially, at age 86. She was too worried about the financial loss since Social Security doesn't exactly match the cost of living, yet, at the same time, the people with whom she worked formed part of her 'external family'; going to work gave her a reason to get up in the morning. I guess, on writing that last sentence, this captures a lot of what retirement is about. You have to set goals for yourself and create a reason for getting up in the morning.

When you were little, you got up to go to school. When you were a little older, you got up to go to work or take care of the children. Now the children have moved out (phfew!) and you don't have to go to work anymore. So, now what?

If you've prepared this correctly, you have the financial security to sit back and decide what you would like to do. If you are reading this and on the brink of retirement and haven't set up your financial aspects, don't count on Social Security to support you. Knowing what you want to do during your retirement and being financially prepared for it are two separate yet key things.

Retirement is something you practically have to start planning for and looking forward to as soon as you finish school. Financial security and planning are not just for the big shots in the executive suite, and making sure that you have a home that you can call your own (and not something that you 'share' with your bank!) is primordial.

So, now you've arrived. You spent 40-plus years of your life thinking, planning for your retirement. What are you going to do with it? The happiest people that I've met are those who are busier now than they were when they were working. Engineers are painting or studying languages, business executives are teaching literacy classes to immigrants, cardiologists are getting their Ph.D.s in history; men who didn't have time to watch their children grow up are participating in their grandchildren's lives – and appreciating it more because there's no stress attached to it. Women who had stayed home to raise their children are creating and running major businesses (but then if they spent thirty years running a household and raising children, running a business is a piece of cake...). Couples who never had time to do anything together are closing their homes for months on end and traveling around the world. People who never showed the slightest artistic ability are having gallery showings of their sculptures or paintings.

The U.S. government finally figured out that people couldn't survive off of their Social Security payments and made it legal to continue working after the normal retirement age. In this case, think about what you would <u>want</u> to do if you needed to supplement your retirement benefits. A retirement occupation can be after school home-care, the crossing guard for a primary school, guardian at a playground or just plain babysitting if you want to be around small children. It can be a librarian's assistant if you want to be surrounded by books. A lot of business people volunteer to help new start-up businesses: young people who have good ideas but don't know how to implement them and need sage executive advice. Just because you retire doesn't mean that your brain stops functioning!

"I was always busy at something. When my daughter was small I had part time jobs or projects. Then I got involved in our town's historical society. At first it was a dozen people meeting in our church hall. I used my event planning knowledge to turn it into a major educational and fund-raising group and to save some of our town's more beautiful, historic homes. It was all volunteer but I got noticed and was offered a full time events marketing job. For more

than 12 years I was running important public events in Washington D.C.

"Retirement wasn't a financial option so when the marketing group I was working for closed, I took a job handling the marketing for a local insurance group. I finally stopped that when I was in my mid-80s. Yes the money was a necessary supplement to my Social Security check but the most important part for me was the human contact. The people in my office were like family."

Peggy
Connecticut, USA

Women who have run households, raised children, helped at school, run the PTA and worked as volunteers all their lives know how to balance their lives using home as their base of operations. One problem with retirement for women, however, is that their housework doesn't go away at age 65. The laundry still has to be done, the groceries purchased, the meals cooked, and the house dusted and cleaned.

"We live in an apartment building with a high percentage of retired couples. Two of my neighbors were big salesmen: one in home products and the other in the automotive industry. Now one is running a local artists' association and the other is the coach of the town's little league soccer team. These people just couldn't image being at home by themselves all the time. They needed to stay busy and intellectually stimulated. They are good examples

to others who sit and wait for something to happen to them."

Cecile

Boulogne, France

Men growing up in the twentieth century associated home as a place to relax, a place to be when they weren't at work. When they retire, they are home full-time and they don't know how to occupy themselves... and they usually end up driving their wives crazy. I know several women who actually rented their husbands corporate suite-style offices, with computers, fax machines and secretaries, just to get them out of the house! Those men were not ready to jump from 8-6 corporate jobs to empty agendas. They needed a sort of half-way house to adjust and slow down.

"My father was glued to the television in the evenings. That was how he relaxed when he came home from work. When he retired, he didn't know what else to do with himself. He read a lot, then he taught literacy classes, he started writing short stories again... and, after telling me for several years that it was a fad that would never last, he discovered the Internet. While he didn't take full advantage of his retirement, he did master the Internet!"

Bill

Ohio, USA

"My husband used to say that when the last of our children finishes university we will retire. I don't think that will be possible financially. What I do hope for is that we will be able to do things

together because we still want to and we have time for ourselves. His plan is that we will still have time to go skiing every year – with and without the kids or grandkids – to visit 'the world' and spend more time with our friends. I hope we'll still be in good enough physical shape to live up to that. It's not just about being financially healthy but also physically healthy!'

Annabelle
Kansas, USA

What do you think? Are you ready to assume now the responsibility for your future; to get organized now so that you can relax later? Have you ever sat down and spoken with your spouse about what he or she might want to do 'later'? Are you sure that you both want the same things out of your good retirement years?

I ask that question because the rest is difficult. Ultimately one of you is going to go first and you need to be mentally prepared to keep going alone. Will you find enough satisfaction from the retirement life that you prepared for together to move ahead if suddenly your life partner isn't standing next to you?

While throughout our lives we struggle with the financial ramifications of our decisions, I think the hardest part might just be coping with the fact that you made all those plans together and you're not sure you want to do them by yourself. If you analyze the situation from a distance you will recognize that the death of your husband or wife shouldn't affect your plans. If you wanted to travel, do it. If you wanted to spend your retirement years perfecting your ballroom dancing techniques, find another partner.

Your life must go on. You should be prepared for this eventuality.

> *"My father remarried almost immediately after mom's death. Why? He couldn't live alone. It wasn't that he couldn't take care of himself, it was just that he didn't want to be alone. I was shocked and a little angry but he was right to do it. It wasn't until much later that I realized just how much my mother was the guiding force in their marriage ...and he needed that."*
>
> Francis
> New Hampshire, USA

Some men really can't be alone, they need the companionship and guidance. Left to themselves, they tend to withdraw from the outside world. On the other hand, I've also met widows who keep themselves busy just waiting to pass on and join their husbands. I suppose that my lovely upstairs neighbor who keeps her husband's ashes in an urn in his office and who regularly sits and talks to him is not alone.

I don't know all the answers. All I know is that, after living a fairly stressful working life, I would like to have the most stress-free retirement that I can create. So I watch and learn. I observe my friends' parents and my parents' friends. I see the people who are happy and those who are not. The stress that we live with every day as working people is reduced because we no longer have to put up with impossible working conditions, angry clients or difficult bosses but the financial stress is ever present.

My husband has a 'don't worry' attitude about retirement but I still worry. There are places on this earth that I want to visit and travelling costs a lot of money…and that's beyond paying the monthly bills and medical care. Financial security really does seem to be the base of a good retirement. Yes, you can develop some illness. Yes, we will all slow down at some point. At age 40 I was already having trouble with my body not keeping up with my mind. At 50 I discovered that silly minor falls from my horse could be horrendously serious, so I can just image what I'll be like at 70 or 80!

Remember I spoke about Gladys, one of the women who mentored me into adulthood? She and her husband lived and worked together as an independent writer/artist team. When her husband, Bernard, died suddenly all their plans to travel, sail, and enjoy their retirement were shattered. An enormous amount of their savings were spent helping Bernard leave this world comfortably and one of his last remarks to her was that she should find a job in a big advertising agency where she would receive medical coverage and retirement benefits.

Gladys sold their beautiful wooden sailboat, she got a smaller apartment in her building, and she got a 'real' job. Gladys was one of those ageless and in the 1980s in America, employers were not allowed to judge someone by their age – let alone ask their age – so Gladys kept working. When major administrative changes were being made in her agency, she finally decided to take her retirement. She had been working almost 18 years since

Bernard's death and had been saving a lot of money. She planned trips, she spent more time at the museums, and she took the time to see friends living outside of New York City. Eighteen months after she retired she was diagnosed with pancreatic cancer and – terrified that she wouldn't be able to afford proper care – she started selling works of art that she and her husband had collected when they were younger.

Her retirement was not as she had planned, but she pulled herself together after Bernard's death and took care of herself. She was 62 (yes, SIXTY-TWO) when she went out and found her first full-time job but she had no choice. Neither of them had family and they never had children to help them out later on. Gladys worked until she was 78. She died two weeks after her 80th birthday. When her estate was settled, there was a little over $3 million – the majority of which she left to a charity. Had her husband lived longer, they would have had trouble keeping up with inflationary cost increases but they would have enjoyed their time together...but it wasn't meant to be. Those are the kinds of things that you can't always anticipate.

Do you need some ideas of how to prepare yourselves financially? Seek advice and don't wait!

There are thousands of ways to prepare yourselves – that's why financial planning is big business; what's important is choosing something that you are comfortable with and planning for the eventualities.

Of course, this comes down to having your life priorities organized; to think carefully about what you want to do with the rest of your life, whether it be your life as a couple or your life by yourself. Remember that retirement doesn't mean that you are getting old. It means that you have achieved a level of security in your life so that you can follow other undiscovered paths. If you have stayed true to your priorities, this is the time in your life that you have been waiting for, planning for, and – because you have taken care of yourself – that you are mentally and physically fit enough to really enjoy.

The advantage of retirement is – though you have given yourself a reason to get out of bed in the morning – if you want to sleep late, you can, as long as the reason is that you are tired because you were busy the day before doing something you really enjoyed.

Conclusion? Seek financial advice early to plan for later. Talk with your partner to blueprint your long term goals. Manage what you *NEED* to do so that you can do what you *WANT* to do!

Life and Death

This is one thing you just can't avoid. People die. Some die after a short period of time; some die after a long period of time. When you lose a close friend or family member do you feel sorry for them or for yourself? Yes, it's sad that they are dying or have died but there isn't anything – most of time – which we, simple mortals, can do about it. What you have to be able to do is pick up the pieces of your own life or your family's life and put them back together as best you can.

You have to, once again, take a look at your basic list of priorities. Are you carrying on with your life? Are you eating, taking a shower, doing the laundry, going to work, walking the dog, taking care of your children if you have them? Are you taking care of the basics?

For many people who have lost someone, day-to-day activities are too heavy a burden to handle. Try to communicate with someone – find some sort of counselor – and try to say the things that you are feeling. After you start the communication process, the priorities come back into focus and you are generally able to continue. You might never be the same person you were.

You will have changed, evolved, matured. This experience might change your priorities. If someone you cared about dearly dies from lung cancer because he smoked too much, it might drive you to stop smoking. You might see that what happened to his family could happen to yours. If you practice a dangerous sport and you lose a sporting buddy in an accident, will it make you more aware of the danger you are taking, and what the repercussions could be for your family's well-being?

One of the things that I became clearly aware of when I had children was my own mortality. Before having children, if something had happened to me it would have been sad for my family but life goes on. No one depended on me. Now that I have children I am keenly aware that they need my presence. Yes, I can be replaced. Another woman can step in and replace my function but no one can replace me as the mother of <u>my</u> children. Nor can my husband ever be replaced as the father of his/our children.

Yes, accidents happen. Trees fall on cars. Cars hit other cars. Until the September 11 attack in America we thought we were safe in our offices but that's no longer true. Airplanes hit office towers. Trains blow-up. Lives change, alter. Your priorities become more focused. You start to reconsider what is important in your life. You start to look at the difference between something that you want and something that you need.

As for many people, the morning came one day when I got a call to pick up my sick daughter from school. When I arrived she was sitting on the edge of a chair in the secretary's waiting room. I could see from the look on her face that she <u>needed</u> a hug. Yes, I had left some important work to go pick her up, and no, I couldn't take her back to the office. She <u>needed</u> to be taken home and tucked into her bed by her mother. Did this cost me anything? No. I was able to keep working at home. Did I get anything out of it? Yes. I was reminded how much my little four-year-old daughter meant to me, and that a hug is sometimes the most valuable thing that I can offer.

What would have happened if I weren't here anymore? Anything. It could have been a nanny or a neighbor or a new mom who came to pick her up. It could have been her father or she could have stayed in the nurse's office until someone picked her up at the end of the day. But she would never have gotten that needed hug from her mom.

The horse accidents I have experienced over the past few years have been clear signs for me that I am still needed. I no longer ride young horses and never, ever ride without a helmet or an air-vest body protection. While I have recovered from head trauma and from broken bones, I can see the impact that these accidents had on my husband and – most notably – my daughter, who also rides. While I tend to believe that you go when it's your 'time', I've stopped tempting the fates and am being much more cautious than before.

Over the years we've been confronted by much life and death experience – in our own lives and those of our friends around us. We lived through a wave of deaths from AIDS among our friends in the 1980s and 1990s, but the closest we came to death (or a near miss) was when our first son was born with a heart defect. His problem was 'minor': two operations and 6 weeks in a pediatric intensive care unit got him on his way to a normal life. However, we met families in the PICU (Pediatric Intensive Care Unit) who were dealing with situations much more serious than our own.

One family that I will never forget had a son, about 5 years old, who was dying of liver cancer. He was close to the end and he knew it, but his parents couldn't accept it yet. They felt they needed to make sure he had all the childhood experiences possible before dying. They arranged for their son to go to the circus – a major event as it meant mobilizing ambulances, doctors and nurses – just so this little boy could see the circus before he died. He didn't really want to go, he had told the nurses so. He was ready to leave this world and go on to another one but his parents couldn't let go. They weren't ready yet. His death actually came as a shock to them, as though they didn't really realize that it would ultimately happen. They kept hoping for a miracle that just didn't arrive.

In another instance while our son was in the PICU, a little girl was brought in who had been hit by a car while out playing. She was being kept alive on life-support systems, but there was little hope. One night we stopped by the hospital late to check on our son and saw all the surgeons waiting around, all dressed in scrubs. The parents of the little girl understood that she was gone and had agreed to allow others to benefit from their loss; a very difficult decisions. The surgeons were all there for organ harvesting.

We met families who were able to take their children home and others who would not have that chance. It made us aware that, while our son's heart defect had altered his life and ours, we would all go on...he would live a virtually normal life. We had lost 6 weeks of being together but that was nothing to the losses of that little boy's or little girl's family.

"Death can be cruel and greedy. Our family had one horrible year in which we lost my older brother and his little daughter. Timothy had a brain tumor when he was about 20. The doctors were able to take it out and he never needed any other treatment. He had finished university and then married a girl he had met while finishing school. They had an adorable little girl, Chrissy. She was just our little Goldilocks...

"That summer, Tim's headaches were back and the doctors had starting treating him with radiotherapy. One summer night when Chrissy was 5, the whole family was at our house for dinner. As people were starting to leave, no one noticed that the little Chrissy was running around in the driveway. Tim's only child was hit and killed in front of our parent's house by a car driven by his wife's sister.

"The emotional blow of losing his daughter was too much for him and he let go. Yes, the cancer had come back but his fight was gone. Unconsciously he must have decided that his place was with his little girl. What he left behind was a grieving family, especially our parents. First the little granddaughter and then their son. Mom aged decades but there were five other children, other grandchildren, and she was a long-term foster mother for two more kids. She kept going.

She managed the day-to-day. Dad was hit hard; he had lost his oldest son. To him there is no sense to it all; he just didn't understand. Nothing could replace his son."

Thomas
Ogden, Utah

Is that what people are looking for when they lose someone: to replace the loss? To fill the void? To occupy themselves with other activities so that they don't have to think?

I've always tried to stand up to death. I realize that it's just another passage in the life we live. I've been sorrowed by the loss of grandparents, seen the death of friends from AIDS as a blessing and an end to their suffering, grieved heavily for a dear friend who committed suicide, and sobbed hopelessly for weeks on end due to the loss of several of my dogs (actually, I'm quite hopeless about the death of my dogs…). But when it comes down to it what we are all looking for is a way to cushion the blow.

Life insurance is a lovely idea. It makes you feel secure. Too bad that all it really does is soften the blow. It's kind of like a car's airbag: It's there, it helped you through a terrible nano-second in your life but the reality of the situation is that your car has been destroyed. Transfer the analogy to a life situation. Yes, you have life insurance. It may help you pay off some debt, but it's not going to replace in any way, shape, or form the person who was insured.

No, I don't have anything against life insurance. It's absolutely vital if you have children because it will assure their immediate future if something happens to you and it will pay for the funeral costs. However, can you honestly say that you do everything you can to avoid having a member of your family actually cash in that insurance policy?

Do you wear a seat belt in your car even when you are 'just driving around the corner to get milk'? Do you always buckle in the children? Do you and the children wear helmets when you are out riding bikes or skating? If you enjoy the thrill of a dangerous sport, do you consider the consequences of your actions on your children if something should go wrong?

As I pointed out earlier, Americans as a whole are more aware of what they have now than they were before September 2001. In countries that have suffered genocide, or terrorists, or tsunamis people are aware that the loss of a family member or close friend can come from nowhere and destabilize their lives. I hope it has made people realize how lucky they really are with what they have, even if it doesn't seem like much from a material standpoint.

Life today is much more precious than we thought. The news media report about shootings, train and plane accidents, and bombings all over the world, but no one takes into account the individual lives anymore: The Person. The individual who won't be going home to his or her children or dog or cat anymore. You need to stop and think. Could it be me?

The two points I'm trying to make here are, first, don't take risks that you don't HAVE to take. Think about your family; think about your responsibilities. Many accidents can be avoided. Second, if you have lost someone dear to you, you must go on. The hard part is finding the strength and courage to do so.

When my friend made the decision to take his own life, I grieved, cried, trembled, and sought answers. After time I was able to understand why and tell him so. I still miss him but understanding helped me find strength and courage to move forward without him. We can all do this. It just takes time…

What conclusions can we draw from this conversation? Well, in a perfect world we should love everyone all the time so we have no regrets when they die. Too bad that's not the real world.

Each person grieves differently. Get help to get through it. Your life goes on and whether you turn to your religion or a friend or a counsellor, do what you *NEED* to do to heal the wound from the loss. No one can say how long it will take. You are stronger than you think. Use that strength to move forward.

Living in Society

Why do we study history?

(Let's pause a moment to think about this question)

Ready?

Here's my answer: I think we study history to learn from the mistakes of those who came before us. At the same time, we also learn the GOOD things that have taken place but the bigger lessons are those that show us mistakes and how to avoid repeating these mistakes in the future.

Did we learn from the mistakes of Napoleon, Khmer Rouge leader Pol Pot, and Hitler (to name a few)? In many cases yes, even though grasping for kingdoms and genocide still continues.

What I think is that none of us spent enough time studying history from, for example, the period of the Crusades. If every human in modern society were to go back and do a detailed study on the Crusades then we might not be so judgmental of others. After all, the

Crusades were about whose religion is better. Amazing, isn't it? A thousand years ago countries were fighting about religion; about protecting the Holy land from infidels. In a thousand years we do not seem to have learned very much.

Many people on our little planet believe that there is a very powerful, knowledgeable 'supreme being' whose laws we must obey; someone who is going to save us when our time comes if we have followed this Being's teachings. No matter how we address this 'Being' or how we pray to it (him or her just don't seem to be the proper pronouns for the Supreme Being) does not matter.

Who has the right to say that his or her Supreme Being is better than someone else's? And why would you actually go to war to prove that your Supreme Being is stronger?

My Supreme Being is not superior to your Supreme Being, or to the Supreme Being of the guy across the street. What is important - what <u>must be respected</u> - is each person's individual right to believe and follow the teachings of his or her personal Supreme Being.

My relationship with MY Supreme Being is a private relationship. What I have to say to and how I treat my Supreme Being has nothing to do with how my neighbor treats his Supreme Being. So why are people all over the world fighting? We have religious freedom. We are not told (in most modern, civilized nations) who we must pray to. We are free to choose! So what gives someone the right to kill the person living in the next region because he thinks his Supreme Being is better than the other guy's?

Interestingly enough, if you look deep down inside every 'modern day' organized religion (Buddhism, Christianity, Hinduism, Islam, Judaism, Sikhism, etc. – and please note alphabetical order not a list based on statistics), they are all PEACEFUL religions. They all teach us to be nice to each other. They teach us that we should try to be the best person possible, to achieve greatness in our lifetimes.

So why are there still religious wars and why are there religious terrorists? Personally I do not know and as we come to the end of this little book of life's priorities I am not going to be able to come up with some magical solution to all the world's issues.

All I can tell you is that if YOU can accept that your relationship with your Supreme Being is your private affair and not bother the person living next door, then you have achieved a high level of wisdom. You have become 'enlightened' as some religions suggest.

One of the things I would like people to have learned to appreciate while reading through this little book is that we must focus on ourselves and our families and ensure that we are advancing, progressing in a forward direction, before concerning ourselves with our neighbors. We all have different priorities! And... why should I have an opinion on my neighbors' priorities? Why should they care about mine?

Is there a conclusion to draw here? Hmmmm… If we, as a group of people, are to continue to inhabit the planet earth (uh, helloooo, we don't have any other options yet…), then we *NEED* to get along better.

If one of the things that we can do is remove anger and derision based on religious views, then I think we should try to do this. Keep your religious opinions to yourself – or rather between you and your Supreme Being. Don't try to impose them on others. We will all live happier and healthier lives together as one society if we do.

I'll try if you will. Is it a deal?

Priorities: On the dawn of a new millennium...

So what are my priorities? To live my life to the best of my abilities. To take care of myself and my husband and my children. To help bring in a salary to improve my family's quality of life but not to the detriment of my or my family's current needs.

Do I feel that I have my priorities in order? Yes, most days I believe that I do. Do I still have a silver pen? Yes, it's in a box somewhere in the back of a closet. Do I carry a fancy leather briefcase? Well, it's leather but I wouldn't call it fancy anymore. I have the same briefcase I started with in 1980 (it was a good buy!). Do I still wear fancy suits and silk scarves? Well, yes, I do but most of them come from the thrift shop, or mega sales at our big department store. I hate buying things full price and would rather buy something 'sustainable' (meaning, something I found at a thrift or consignment shop...)

Technology? Yes, I have an iPhone and an iPad. This is one of the joys of the twenty-first century. I can stay in touch with work and family from pretty much everywhere. I don't bring my computer home unless it is absolutely necessary, but I do bring my iPad so that I can keep working from home if I need to, or while sitting in the snack bar at the sports club waiting for one of the kids.

I don't *need* these 'tools' but I *want* to make my life easier and I also want to stay in touch with my kids and my mom wherever they are. Yes, I could live without them but right now, in this instant consumer world, if my kids or a close friend or family member need to reach me, they can.

So what I have been writing about? All these little stories are life decisions. Before mass media, before the Internet, before television and radio, before the telephone, before what we call now 'modern times,' how did people transmit their messages? Our ancestors told us stories. They told us about the life adventures of their friends and their ancestors. The stories they told us had a function, a moral. We listened to them and we learned from them. We took out of each story what we needed to form our 'selves', our personalities and our proper priorities.

No one really takes the time to sit down and <u>listen</u> anymore; no one seems to take the time to reflect on what's going on around us. Well, perhaps that has changed since September 11, 2001. That is the day that America grew up, and maybe the whole world. '9-11' made us look at what was important. That's what I've been trying to do here; to give you the little stories that your ancestors wanted to tell you and to remind you to keep an eye on your priorities.

Each person will take from this what he or she wants. Some may find it frivolous and redundant. (Sorry.) Some may find profound resolve. That would be great. Some may simply remember what it's like to have a hug from their little girl when she wasn't feeling well and remember that it was just as great a hug for the little girl as it was for her mother or father.

But what I've been trying to do is show you how to find _your life_'s priorities; to be able to make important decisions about *what you want* and *what you need* through communication, reflection, and finding the truths in your life.

Good luck!

Something to think about...

A wise old professor sat before his students with some items in front of him. The students had come before this man because they were in the last few days of their philosophy studies in university. When everyone was seated and attentive, he wordlessly picked up a large empty jar, placed it before him and proceeded to fill it with rocks about two inches in diameter right up to the top. He asked if the jar was full. They all agreed that it was.

The professor then picked up a box of pebbles and poured them into the jar. He shook the jar slightly. The pebbles, of course, rolled into the open areas between the rocks. The students laughed.

He asked his students again if the jar was now full and they agreed that, yes, it was.

The professor then picked up a box of sand and poured it into the jar. Of course, the sand filled up the jar even further. The students did not laugh.

He asked his students again if the jar was now full and they did not answer but simply stared back at him.

"*Now,*" said the professor, "*I want you to recognize that this jar represents your lives. The rocks are important things: your family, your partner, your health, your children; anything that is so important to you that if it were lost, you would be nearly destroyed.*

"*The pebbles are the other things in life that matter, but on a smaller scale. The pebbles represent your job, your house, your car.*

"*The sand is everything else. The small stuff.*

"*If you put the sand or the pebbles into the jar first, there is no room for the rocks. The same goes for your life. If you spend all your energy and time on the small stuff, material things, you will never have room for the things that are truly important.*

"*Pay attention to the things that are critical in your life. Play with your children. Take your partner out dancing. There will always be time to go to work, clean the house, give a dinner party, and fix the garbage disposal. Take care of the rocks first – the things that really matter.*"

Then the professor picked up a pitcher of water and poured it into the jar. Of course, the water filled up the jar and even a few drops escaped on to the table.

"*Water represents your soul, your emotion. It's what connects all of the important things in your life. It's what makes you believe that you can do anything and that everything is possible. It is what holds you together just as it now binds the sand to the pebbles and the pebbles to the rocks. You can't live without it and it can't work without you."*

Set your priorities: the rest is just pebbles and sand.

Something to do...

A few years ago, while cleaning out my closet in my parents' house, I found a list I wrote in 1980. It was a list of things that I wanted to do with my life.

Its presence surprised me since I have no recollection of writing it. It wasn't long; it wasn't profound. It was just a list of things that I thought I would like to accomplish before I grew up.

Have I accomplished these things? Surprisingly enough yes. What is interesting is that I knew myself well enough 35 some odd years ago to anticipate my adult life and that I haven't varied from these plans (which is actually what surprised me the most).

When I married my husband I didn't remember having made the previous decision to marry someone who had brothers and sisters. When my husband and I decided together to move to France to raise our children I had no recollection that I had written on a scrap of paper that someday I wanted to live in Europe.

There are less than ten items on my list but all of them I can happily and proudly say that I have accomplished. This is not to say that my life is complete…over the years I have added things to my life list but I'm pleased to know that I'm on track.

Now it's your turn.

Make your list. Look inside of yourself and decide what you want to do before you grow up (even if you think you are grown up…). Be truthful and write what are really *YOUR* priorities.

Now take that list and put it somewhere you will find it in about twenty years or so. Leave it with your will in a safety deposit box, or in a drawer where you keep special things, or do what I did, stuff it inside a handbag that you always loved but don't use very often (and one that you refuse to give away).

You'll find your list again someday. I hope that you will be as pleasantly surprised as I was; that you are pleased with the life that you chose and the course in life that you've taken.

It is, after all, based on your priorities!

CPSIA information can be obtained
at www.ICGtesting.com
Printed in the USA
FFOW01n0941230415
12866FF